W9-AOJ-413

Lakota and
Cheyenne

Lakota and Cheyenne

Indian Views
of the Great Sioux War,
1876–1877

Compiled, Edited, and Annotated
by Jerome A. Greene

WITHDRAWN

University of Oklahoma Press : Norman and London

By Jerome A. Greene

Evidence and the Custer Enigma (Kansas City, 1973)
Slim Buttes, 1876: An Episode of the Great Sioux War (Norman, 1982)
Yellowstone Command: Colonel Nelson A. Miles and the Great Sioux War, 1876–1877 (Lincoln, 1991)
Battles and Skirmishes of the Great Sioux War, 1876–1877: The Military View (Norman, 1993)
Lakota and Cheyenne: Indian Views of the Great Sioux War, 1876–1877 (Norman, 1994)

This book is published with the generous assistance of the Mellon Humanities Publications Fund.

Library of Congress Cataloging-in-Publication Data

Lakota and Cheyenne : Indian views of the Great Sioux War, 1876–1877 / compiled, edited, and annotated by Jerome A. Greene.
    p.   cm.
    Includes index.
    ISBN: 0–8061–2681–7
    1. Dakota Indians—Wars, 1876.   2. Cheyenne Indians—Wars, 1876.   3. Teton Indians—Wars. I. Greene, Jerome A.
E83.876.L25   1994
973.8'2—dc20
                                  94–12473
                                      CIP

1 2 3 4 5 6 7 8 9 10

For My Children

Contents

CONTENTS

Illustrations

Map

Acknowledgments

R. ELI PAUL, Nebraska State Historical Society; Douglas C. McChristian, Little Bighorn Battlefield National Monument; Paul L. Hedren, Fort Union Trading Post National Historic Site; Michael Wagner, Southwest Museum, Los Angeles; Robert M. Utley, Moose, Wyoming; Richard A. Fox, Jr., University of South Dakota, Vermillion; John D. McDermott, Sheridan, Wyoming; Douglas D. Scott, National Park Service Midwest Archeological Center, Lincoln, Nebraska; Margot Liberty, Sheridan, Wyoming; L. Clifford Soubier, Charles Town, West Virginia; Harry H. Anderson, Milwaukee County Historical Society, Milwaukee, Wisconsin; Robert G. Pilk, National Park Service, Denver; Thomas R. Buecker, Fort Robinson State Museum, Crawford, Nebraska; Paula Fleming, Smithsonian Institution, Washington, D.C.; Lawrence F. Van Horn, National Park Service, Denver; Harry Burke and Lula Red Cloud, Hermosa, South Dakota; Joseph C. Porter, Fort Worth, Texas; and the staffs of the National Archives, Washington, D.C.; the Nebraska State Historical Society; the Harold B. Lee Library, Brigham Young University, Provo, Utah; the South Dakota State Historical Society, Pierre; Scotts Bluff National Monument, Scottsbluff, Nebraska; the Montana Historical Society, Helena; the North Dakota State Historical Society; and the Western History Collections, University of Oklahoma Libraries.

Introduction
The Great Sioux War
and Indian Testimony
By Jerome A. Greene

THE GREAT SIOUX WAR comprised a series of sequential battles and skirmishes that arrayed elements of the U.S. Army against diverse tribes of Teton, or western, Sioux and Northern Cheyenne Indians during a period of fifteen months from March 1876 through May 1877. The conflict embraced fifteen encounters of varying magnitude that ranged across an extensive landscape encompassing parts of present-day Montana, Wyoming, Nebraska, and South Dakota. The war evolved from the inexorable movement of whites onto lands claimed by the Sioux and Cheyennes (as well as other tribes) on the northern Great Plains. Its conclusion saw the intertribal coalition sundered, its people scattered among reservations in Dakota Territory, Nebraska, and the Indian Territory (present Oklahoma) or refuged in Canada.

The two tribes involved in the Great Sioux War, the Teton Sioux, or Lakotas, and the Northern Cheyennes, while linguistically unrelated, nonetheless possessed cultural similarities that had influenced their parallel courses by the mid-1870s. The Algonkian-speaking Cheyennes, once inhabitants of the country adjoining the western Great Lakes, had been drawn by the buffalo herds to occupy the prairie country east of the Missouri River late in the seventeenth century. Augmented by the arrival of horses among them, their westward migration continued, and within a few decades the Cheyennes hunted beyond the Black Hills as far north as the Yellowstone River and as far south as the Platte. By the early nineteenth century, the tribe had divided into northern and southern segments that nevertheless maintained band and familial interrelationships. In their seasonal movements, Cheyenne warriors vied with other Indian tribes for supremacy of the land and its game resources. The Cheyennes became noted fighters as a result of their battles with neighboring tribes, especially the Crows, Kiowas, Comanches, and bitterly hated Pawnees. Conversely, they formed durable alliances with other groups, notably the linguistically related Arapahoes and the culturally like Teton tribes, and particularly the Oglalas.

The Tetons, formerly prairie tribesmen, had reached the plains country traversing over much the same ground as the Cheyennes, and during the same approximate period. The seven tribes of the Siouan-speaking Tetons— Oglalas, (Those Who Scatter Their Own Grain), Hunkpapas, (Campers at the Entrance of the Camp Circle), Sichangus (Burned Thighs People, commonly known as Brulés), Minneconjous (Planters By the Water), Sihasapas (Blackfeet, or Wearers of Black Moccasins), Oohenunpa (Two Kettles, or Two Boilings People), and Itazipchos (Those Without Bows, commonly called Sans Arcs)—occupied the Yellowstone region early in the nineteenth century, laying a strong claim by virtue of superior numbers. Although the Sioux and Cheyennes occasionally fought one another, their conflicts were minimal compared to those between the Sioux and the Crows, who vigorously contested Sioux encroachment. The Lakotas and Cheyennes shared common objectives, including security; intermarriages and increasing cultural affinity fostered intertribal cohesiveness that in no way compromised either tribe's autonomy.

Because of their relatively large population, the Teton Sioux attracted the attention of whites during the period of national expansion that preceded the Civil War. Treaties arranged with the Plains tribes in 1851 eventually promoted conflict between the Sioux and the U.S. government. Bloodshed intermittently occurred until the late 1860s, most of it involving Sioux attacks on gold-seekers and troops who invaded their country. In 1868, the government and some of the Lakota bands concluded the Fort Laramie treaty, which created the Great Sioux Reservation in what is now western South Dakota. Some of the Lakotas, however, particularly the followers of Sitting Bull, Crazy Horse, and other chiefs, refused to sign the treaty and avoided the reservation altogether. Furthermore, many of the Indians who had agreed to reside on the reservation now opted to join their kinsmen in the north on a seasonal basis.

Two events finally culminated in the Great Sioux War. First, a surveying expedition for the Northern Pacific Railroad penetrated into the Yellowstone River lands inhabited by the northern Sioux in the summer of 1873. Second, in 1874 the confirmation of gold in the Black Hills provoked a rush of miners onto the Great Sioux Reservation. Both events symbolized the expansive designs of white Americans, so far as Indian rights were concerned, while signaling to their government the need to forestall conflict with the Sioux over the coveted lands.

The Indians reacted defensively, attacking parties of miners in the vicinity of the Black Hills while striking camps of tribes friendly to the United States. Late in 1875, the government ordered all Lakotas then beyond the boundary of the Great Sioux Reservation, including the nontreaty followers of Sitting Bull and Crazy Horse, to place themselves within its confines. If they did not come to the agencies, troops would be sent to force them in. Freezing conditions prevented many tribesmen from learning of the directive; doubtless many would not have complied anyway. In sum, none of the targeted bands in the Yellowstone country responded, and the War Department initiated a winter campaign against them.

The war that followed was unwanted by the Indians, who desired to be left alone to continue their traditional way of life. First to come under attack by U.S. troops was a village of Northern Cheyennes that stood along the Powder River in southeastern Montana Territory and mistakenly was thought by the army to contain Sioux. On March 17, 1876, an army column struck these people at dawn, driving them from their homes, seizing their ponies, and destroying their supplies. But the warriors countered, retrieved their animals, and suffered but minimal casualties in the fighting. Far from succeeding, the army attack at Powder River only solidified the Cheyennes' alliance with the Tetons and steeled their resolve. As such, from both Indian and military perspectives, the Powder River battle was a critical beginning.

Emboldened by the onset of fighting, the Sioux and Cheyennes anticipated army movements over the next several months and, confident in their success, initiated combat against the troops. On June 9, 1876, warriors briefly attacked Brigadier General George Crook's bivouac along the upper Tongue River, firing on the soldiers from bluffs above the stream. Eight days later, more than one thousand warriors struck Crook's command on Rosebud Creek, besting the army in a day-long encounter that raged across several square miles of terrain. Significantly, the Indians drove Crook south, away from other military columns operating in the region.

By June 25, a village containing perhaps 8,000 people—Lakotas representing all the seven tribes, plus Northern Cheyennes accompanied by some of their southern kinsmen and a few Arapahoes and eastern Sioux—had located in the Little Big Horn Valley, one stream west of Rosebud Creek. The Indians, now increasingly drawn together for security, had assembled in a favored spot known to the Sioux as Greasy Grass to hunt and to pursue traditional religious activities. When troops under Lieu-

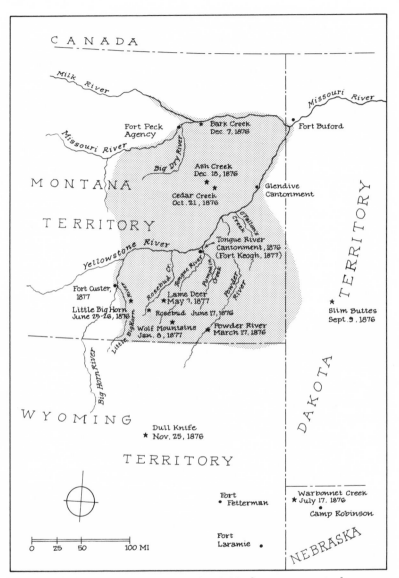

Area of the Great Sioux War, 1876–1877, showing principal zone
of activity and locations of major battles and skirmishes.

tenant Colonel George A. Custer struck the village at midday, as many as 2,500 warriors countered, destroying that officer's immediate command of approximately 225 men and forcing the other battalions to seek refuge on the bluffs overlooking the river until the tribesmen withdrew. The Little Big Horn victory was complete and resounding; it raised the confidence of the Lakota-Cheyenne union and demoralized the army. Today, Little Big Horn—the major Indian triumph in the Great Sioux War—remains the best known of all engagements of the conflict. Because of the mystery surrounding the demise of Custer's immediate command, the Little Big Horn has assumed legendary stature. Indian eyewitness reports thus are critical to understanding what occurred during Custer's phase of the battle.

A long period of military retribution followed the Indian victory at Little Big Horn. None of the subsequent engagements assumed that battle's scale, but their cumulative impact, coupled with the near starvation of the Indians, effectively destroyed the tribesmen's unity and drove most to yield to the government. With few exceptions, army-Indian encounters after Little Big Horn consisted of widely scattered actions in which troops defeated piecemeal the once powerful Indian alliance.

Early in July a combined party of Sioux and Cheyennes clashed with a scouting party from Crook's command and almost succeeded in preventing their escape. Later that month, a band of Cheyennes who had left Red Cloud Agency to join the warring factions in the north ran headlong into an army column patrolling northeast of Fort Laramie. After an encounter with the troops in which one of their number was killed, the Indians retreated to the agency, pursued all the way by the soldiers. The first major setback to the Indians in the Great Sioux War, however, came in September, when a village of Lakotas and Cheyennes was assaulted by a battalion of Crook's command.

Most of the people fled in the misty dawn. A few found shelter in a ravine but were forced to surrender. The Battle of Slim Buttes, occurring within the confines of the Sioux reservation, forecast the destruction and despair that visited the tribesmen over the remaining eight months.

Indians who returned north to hunt buffalo in the autumn of 1876 found that a permanent military presence had been established with construction of an army cantonment at the mouth of Tongue River on the Yellowstone. They reacted angrily, striking an army supply train en route to the new post. After the post's commander, Colonel Nelson A. Miles, failed to negotiate Sitting Bull's surrender in a face-to-face meeting, he ordered his troops to attack the Indians at Cedar Creek, north of the Yellowstone. Although Sitting Bull fled with his immediate followers, several hundred Indians ultimately yielded to Miles. But of these, only a small body actually went to the agencies; most continued hunting to sustain themselves and their families and to prolong their freedom.

Throughout the winter of 1876–77 the troops kept pressure on the tribesmen. In November and December, Sitting Bull's people sought relief from tribes situated near the Fort Peck Indian Agency along the Missouri River. But the soldiers soon arrived. During the latter month, part of Miles's command skirmished with the Indians along the Missouri, and on December 18 the troops attacked Sitting Bull's camp of 122 lodges along Ash Creek. The occupants of the village were driven into the freezing elements without their property; thereafter, Sitting Bull's influence faded among the Lakotas. Eventually, he led his band into Canada, where he remained until 1881.

While the Lakotas north of the Yellowstone contended with the army, the Northern Cheyennes under Dull Knife suffered a crippling defeat in Wyoming that largely ended their involvement in the war. On November 25, 1876, more than two hundred lodges of Cheyennes—

some fifteen hundred Indians—nestled in a canyon of the Big Horn Mountains, were attacked by a command under Colonel Ranald S. Mackenzie. In one of the largest battles of the war, Mackenzie's troopers stormed the encampment at dawn, chasing families into the cold and capturing horses and property. The warriors fought back futilely; in the end, at least forty of them died. The Cheyenne families trekked north seeking help from Crazy Horse's Oglalas in the Tongue River region of southern Montana Territory. Many women and children did not survive the journey. Others, facing the reality of their weakened condition, turned themselves in at the Nebraska agencies during the next few months.

For the Indians, the winter of 1876–77 only grew worse. Their condition desperate, they continued to challenge the soldiers. On January 8, Crazy Horse's Sioux, augmented by Northern Cheyennes, confronted Miles in the upper Tongue River valley. Desiring to protect their nearby village, the Indians assaulted the troops early in the morning and kept up the fight until a blizzard obscured the belligerents from each other. The warriors withdrew up the Tongue, while the soldiers returned to their cantonment. Although both sides sustained minimal losses, the Battle of Wolf Mountains alerted the tribesmen to the hopelessness of holding out longer. Factionalism appeared to further erode their unity, and, much like the vanquished Cheyennes from Dull Knife's camp, the Oglalas and other Lakota tribesmen began to surrender in large numbers.

In a last bid for freedom, a band of Minneconjou Lakotas under Lame Deer determined to remain afield. After most of the Indians had either turned themselves in to Miles or had started for the agencies, Lame Deer and his people—some sixty-odd lodges with approximately 430 occupants—turned towards the upper Rosebud and in early May 1877 camped along Muddy Creek, a tributary of that stream. Most of the people were asleep at daybreak on

May 7 when Miles's soldiers charged the tepees, killed Lame Deer and thirteen other Minneconjous, and chased the rest into the surrounding hills. Over the summer, the survivors, pursued by troops, traveled to the Nebraska agencies. On May 6, the day before Miles destroyed Lame Deer's village, Crazy Horse led almost 900 Sioux men, women, and children into Camp Robinson, Nebraska. Four months later, on September 5, the Oglala leader was mortally wounded in a scuffle at the post guardhouse. Together with Sitting Bull's passage into Canada, Crazy Horse's death symbolized the conclusion of the largest Indian war in American history.

This book presents the recollections of Lakota and Cheyenne veterans of the various engagements of the Great Sioux War. It complements a previous volume by affording an Indian viewpoint and thereby facilitating a greater understanding of events and on-site intercultural dynamics regarding Sioux War battlefields.[1] Most of these accounts have not been previously published. They offer both immediate testimony, that given within weeks or months of an event, and reminiscent testimony, that given years or decades later, often to scholarly minded interrogators.

Indian testimony, ostensibly a valuable adjunct in determining the history of Indian-white relations, must at the outset be considered with care. Obviously there existed a language problem, in that an informant's remarks, almost always translated from Lakota or Cheyenne (or even gesture or sign language) into English, created a filtering process that, especially in the early days, was prone to error. Equally troublesome, statements rendered in the first person, processed through an interpreter, were usually transcribed into the third person by the receiver. Some questioners rearranged the substance of accounts before their transcription, further jeopardizing their accuracy. There are other faults, too. Because of the war honors tradition of Plains tribal cultures, battle accounts were very individualistic, reflecting the personal character of Plains warfare, and thus seldom promoted perspectives of group behavior in combat. Further, the Indian record described events as the people remembered them; errors of perception were always possible, and to this extent such sources must be accepted with certain faith, for there is often no means of verification.

Because of these inherent problems, Indian testimony has been dismissed, or at best reluctantly accepted, by most historians. Today it is apparent, however, that its pluses outweigh its minuses. Indian testimony, carefully weighed, exhibits advantages that make it a valid tool for assessing the past. Veracity was important in tribal society, and so was memory. Remembering such minute data was instilled as part of Indian storytelling ritual, wherein the storyteller was culturally obliged to relate an event accurately, consequently ensuring its perpetuation by future generations. Because of its individualistic character, the Indian record is often most useful in recalling personal incidents that occurred during encounters with whites rather than in describing broader aspects. For example, the many native statements about the Little Big Horn often corroborate each other in details of the struggle while differing materially on more contextual facets.

If this sense of accuracy, born of cultural affinity, is the constant that validates Indian testimony, it must overcome biases that have traditionally neutralized its value, notably among non-Indians. Perhaps the biggest hurdle, as previously noted, is the translation factor; if errors of interpretation occurred, so, quite likely, did errors of fact and feeling. Moreover, sometimes words and phrases interpreted might not convey the literal meaning intended by the informant. This was noticeably the case for spatial and temporal matters; time and distance measurements and geographical descriptions often emerged from the accounts as confusing benchmarks. Consequently, Indian assertions might not be altogether precise and must be evaluated with some latitude if they are to benefit overall knowledge of these battles.

Both types of Indian statements can be valuable. Reminiscent testimony, by its distance from an event, was more often bias-free for both giver and receiver than testimony delivered soon afterwards. This observation is especially true of accounts of the Little Big Horn, wherein surrendering Sioux and Cheyennes, hurriedly pressed for information of that battle, became intimidated by virtue of their recent involvement there. Fearing retribution, they either subordinated their personal roles or told what they believed their questioners wanted to hear. On the other hand, immediate accounts, if indeed forthright, can be rich sources for details over reminiscent accounts sometimes executed decades later.

As mentioned, most immediate accounts dealt with the Custer fight; few Sioux or Cheyennes were interviewed about other battles and skirmishes of 1876–77. Conversely, many reminiscent statements brought forth years later described these seemingly less provocative engagements, as well as the Custer fight, because both amateur and professional students of Indian history took more interest and had ample opportunity to gain the Indian perspective about them. So far as the Little Big Horn goes, both immediate and reminiscent Indian recollections are inordinately significant in depicting what happened on Custer's battlefield. Comparisons of reports about that encounter disclose surprising analogies in their contents about Custer's route to destruction. Regarding other Sioux War engagements, Indian recollections, taken together with military accounts, contribute to a more comprehensive knowledge about them.

Despite the obvious pitfalls that accompany the employment of Indian testimony (non-Indian testimony also has its problems), it nevertheless merits attention. The selections in this book represent a fairly comprehensive record of the engagements of the Great Sioux War as described by Teton Sioux and Northern Cheyenne eyewitnesses. Brevity in the Indian recollections, as well as the availability of a variety of largely unused sources, has dictated that, for each engagement, several accounts be presented. Internal nuances, as well as the knowledge of who conducted an interview and under what circumstances, often suggested which accounts were more objective than others, and this proved to be a selecting factor. The presentations are true eyewitness accounts, not hearsay, that provide clear renditions of the battle actions. (In the case of the Cedar Creek encounter, the immediate accounts used are limited in detail regarding the fighting; also, no Indian account of the fight at Ash Creek, Montana, on December 18, 1876, wherein Sitting Bull's village was destroyed, has been located.) Because of their accuracy and availability, there are more reminiscent accounts than immediate ones in this volume.

In preparing these statements for publication, faithfulness to the original material was the utmost guiding principle. A few of the accounts have been published elsewhere and are identified as such; most, however, have not previously appeared in print and have been drawn verbatim from reports and manuscripts of the recipients of the accounts. In either case, editorial changes have been kept to a minimum. As required or appropriate, punctuation has occasionally been added to improve readability. Also, some words, names, and terms abbreviated in the transcriptions have been completed to further promote clarity. In no way has the substance of the accounts been altered, except to indicate in brackets or footnotes wherever appropriate obvious errors of fact. And wherever interview content lapsed into the irrelevant, it is omitted and its omission indicated by use of ellipses.

For Further Reading

Bad Heart Bull, Amos, and Blish, Helen H. *A Pictographic History of the Oglala Sioux*. Lincoln: University of Nebraska Press, 1967.

Graham, William A. (comp.). *The Custer Myth: A Source Book of Custeriana*. Harrisburg, Pa.: The Stackpole Company, 1953.

Greene, Jerome A. *Evidence and the Custer Enigma: A Reconstruction of Indian-Military History*. Kansas City: The Lowell Press, 1973.

———. *Slim Buttes, 1876: An Episode of the Great Sioux War*. Norman: University of Oklahoma Press, 1982.

———. *Yellowstone Command: Colonel Nelson A. Miles and the Great Sioux War, 1876–1877*. Lincoln: University of Nebraska Press, 1991.

Hammer, Kenneth (ed.). *Custer in '76: Walter Camp's Notes on the Custer Fight*. Provo, Utah: Brigham Young University Press, 1976.

Hardorff, Richard G. (comp., ed.). *Lakota Recollections of the Custer Fight: New Sources of Indian-Military History*. Spokane: The Arthur H. Clark Company, 1991.

Hedren, Paul L. *Fort Laramie in 1876: Chronicle of a Frontier Post at War*. Lincoln: University of Nebraska Press, 1988.

Howard, James H. *The Warrior Who Killed Custer: The Personal Narrative of Chief Joseph White Bull*. Lincoln: University of Nebraska Press, 1968.

Hyde, George E. *Red Cloud's Folk: A History of the Oglala Sioux Indians*. Norman: University of Oklahoma Press, 1937.

———. *Spotted Tail's Folk: A History of the Brule Sioux*. Norman: University of Oklahoma Press, 1961.

Kadlecek, Edward, and Kadlecek, Mabell. *To Kill an Eagle: Indian Views on the Last Days of Crazy Horse*. Boulder, Colo.: Johnson Publishing Company, 1981.

Marquis, Thomas B. *Keep the Last Bullet for Yourself: The True Story of Custer's Last Stand*. New York: Two Continents Publishing Group, 1976.

Smith, Sherry L. *The View from Officers' Row: Army Perceptions of Western Indians*. Tucson: University of Arizona Press, 1990.

Stands in Timber, John, and Liberty, Margot. *Cheyenne Memories*. New Haven: Yale University Press, 1967.

Utley, Robert M. *Frontier Regulars: The United States Army and the Indian, 1866–1891*. New York: The Macmillan Company, 1973.

————. *The Indian Frontier of the American West, 1846–1890*. Albuquerque: University of New Mexico Press, 1984.

Vestal, Stanley. *New Sources of Indian History, 1850–1891*. Norman: University of Oklahoma Press, 1934.

Lakota and
Cheyenne

Chapter 1
The Battle of Powder River, March 17, 1876

Wooden Leg, Northern Cheyenne; Black Eagle, Northern Cheyenne; Kate Bighead, Northern Cheyenne; and Iron Hawk, Hunkpapa Lakota

Late in the winter of 1875–76, a body of Northern Cheyennes out hunting from Red Cloud Agency camped along the Powder River in southeastern Montana Territory. Unimpressed by the directive ordering tribesmen to the reservation, the Indians watched for the troops that they heard had been sent into the region. In fact, an army commanded by Brigadier General George Crook had marched north from Fort Fetterman, Wyoming Territory, in early March 1876 in a movement that provoked the first engagement of the Great Sioux War.

On March 17, approximately 400 soldiers from Crook's command attacked the Powder River village of sixty-five lodges under Chief Old Bear. The camp probably contained 450 Indians, including as many as 150 warriors and other combatants. The troops presumed that the village contained Oglala Lakotas—Crazy Horse's Sioux—and by coincidence a small body of Sioux were camped nearby. But the assault mainly affected the Cheyennes, driving them from their lodges, which were captured along with a large herd of ponies. Late in the day the Cheyennes counterattacked, successfully retrieving their horses after the troops withdrew from the burning encampment. This initial clash produced minimal casualties on either side, but set the tone for the war that followed and solidified the Cheyenne-Lakota alliance for mutual security.

The Northern Cheyenne warrior Wooden Leg provided the following account of the Powder River battle, in which he participated as a young man of eighteen years, to Dr. Thomas B. Marquis, a former agency physician to the Northern Cheyennes, during the 1920s. It is one of the few Indian accounts of

3

Powder River known to exist and is easily the most comprehensive and detailed. Wooden Leg, who served as a principal informer of Cheyenne culture and history to Marquis, was a veteran of numerous clashes with the soldiers in 1876 and 1877, including the Battle of the Little Big Horn. His recollections were corroborated by other Cheyennes interviewed by Marquis, and their remembrances augmented Wooden Leg's memories. The account is excerpted from Marquis, A Warrior Who Fought Custer (Minneapolis: Midwest Company, 1931).

OUR CAMP WAS MOVED to a point just above where Little Powder river flows into Powder river and on the west side of the larger stream. The soldiers went over the hills to the headwaters of Hanging Woman creek. They followed this stream down to Tongue river. We felt safe then. Many of our people thought they were not seeking us at all.

But one day some Cheyennes hunting antelope at the head of Otter creek, just over the hills west from our camp, saw the soldiers camped there. The hunters urged their horses back to warn us. Some of the horses became exhausted in the run, so their riders had to come on afoot. A herald notified the people. All was excitement. The council of old men appointed ten young men to go out that night and watch the movements of the soldiers. Others were out scouting or were awake and watching, but these ten had the special duty. Most of the people slept, feeling secure under the protection of the appointed outer sentinels. Early in the morning an old man arose and went to the top of a nearby knoll to observe or to pray, as old men were in the habit of doing. He had been there only a few moments when he began shouting toward the camp:

"The soldiers are right here! The soldiers are right here!"

Already the attacking white men were between the horse herd and the camp. The ten scouts during the hours of darkness and storm had missed meeting the soldiers.

Wooden Leg, Northern Cheyenne, 1920s. Courtesy of the Smithsonian Institution, National Anthropological Archives.

They found a trail, this trail going up the creek valley. They turned their horses and whipped them in the effort to get ahead of the invaders. But the tired horses played out. They did not catch up with the soldiers until these had arrived at the camp, or afterward.

Women screamed. Children cried for their mothers. Old people tottered and hobbled away to get out of reach of the bullets singing among the lodges. Braves seized whatever weapons they had and tried to meet the attack. I owned a muzzle-loading rifle, but I had no bullets for it. I owned also a cap-and-ball six shooter, but I had loaned it to Star, a cousin who was one of the ten special scouts of the night before. In turn, he had let me have bow and arrows he had borrowed from Puffed Cheek. My armament then consisted of this bow and arrows belonging to Puffed Cheek.

I skirted around afoot to get at our horse herd. I looped my lariat rope over the neck of the first convenient one. It belonged to Old Bear, the old man chief of our band. But just now it became my war pony. I quickly made a lariat bridle and mounted the recovered animal. A few other Cheyennes did the same as I had done. But most of them remained afoot. I shot arrows at the soldiers. Our people had not much else to shoot. Only a few had guns and also ammunition for them.

All of the soldiers who first appeared had white horses. Another band of them who charged soon afterward from another direction had only bay horses. I started back to try to get to my home lodge. I wanted my shield, my other medicine objects and whatever else I might be able to carry away. Women were struggling along burdened with packs of precious belongings. Some were dragging or carrying their children. All were shrieking in fright. I came upon one woman who had a pack on her back, one little girl under an arm and an older girl clinging to her free right hand. She was crying, both of the girls were crying, and all three of them were almost exhausted. They had just dived into a thicket for a rest when I rode up to them. It was Last Bull's wife and their two daughters.

"Let me take one of the children," I proposed.

The older girl, age about ten years, was lifted up behind me. A little further on I picked up also an eight-year-old boy who was trudging along behind a mother carrying on her back a baby and under her arms two other children. The girl behind me clasped her arms about my waist. I wrapped an arm about the boy in front of me. With my free arm and hand I guided my horse as best I could. The animal too was excited by the tumult. It shied and plunged. But I got the two children out of danger. Then I went back to help in the fight.

Two Moons, Bear Walks on a Ridge and myself were together. We centered an attack upon one certain soldier. Two Moons had a repeating rifle. As we stood in concealment he stood it upon end in front of him and passed his hands up and down the barrel, not touching it, while making medicine. Then he said: "My medicine is good; watch me kill that soldier." He fired, but his bullet missed. Bear Walks on a Ridge then fired his muzzle-loading rifle. His bullet hit the soldier in the back of the head. We rushed upon the man and beat and stabbed him to death. Another Cheyenne joined us to help in the killing. He took the soldier's rifle. I stripped off the blue coat and kept it. Two Moons and Bear Walks on a Ridge took whatever else he had and they wanted.

One Cheyenne was killed by the soldiers. Another had his forearm badly shattered. Braided Locks, who is yet living, had the skin of one cheek furrowed by a bullet. The Cheyennes were beaten away from the camp. From a distance we saw the destruction of our village. Our tepees were burned, with everything in them except what the soldiers may have taken. Extra flares at times showed the explosion of powder, and there was the occasional pop of a cartridge from the fires. The Cheyennes were rendered very poor. I had nothing left but the clothing I had on, with the soldier coat added. My eagle wing bone flute, my medicine pipe, my rifle, everything else of mine, were gone.

This was in the last part of the winter. Melted snow water was running everywhere. We waded across the Powder river and set off to the eastward. All of the people

except some of the warriors were afoot. The few young
men on horseback stayed behind to guard the other people
as they got away. One old woman, a blind person, was
missing. All others were present except the Cheyenne
who had been killed.

The soldiers did not follow us. That night we who had
horses went back to see what had become of them. At the
destroyed camp we saw one lodge still standing. We went
to it. There was the missing old blind woman. Her tepee
and herself had been left entirely unharmed. We talked
about this matter, all agreeing that the act showed the
soldiers had good hearts.

We found the soldier camp. We found also our horses
they had taken. We crept toward the herd, out a little
distance from the camp. One Cheyenne would whisper, "I
see my horse." Another would say, "There is mine." Some
could not see their own, but they took whichever ones
they could get. I got my own favorite animal. We made
some effort then to steal some of the horses of the white
men. But they shot at us, so we went away with the part of
our own herd that we could manage. When we returned
with them and caught up with our people we let the
women and some of the old people ride. I gave then to
Chief Old Bear his horse I had captured when the soldiers
first attacked us. He said, "Thank you, my friend," and he
gave the horse to his woman while he kept on afoot.

*Another Northern Cheyenne, Black Eagle, remembered the
Powder River fighting in an account given to anthropologist
George Bird Grinnell in 1907. It is in Notebook 347, George
Bird Grinnell Collection, Braun Research Library, Southwest
Museum, Los Angeles.*

[THE CHEYENNES] MOVED over on Powder River. The
grass was now up. Cheyenne young men from camp were
out from camp traveling about and saw many soldiers

going up Otter Creek. There were many of them. The young men took the news back to camp that soldiers were coming and wished them to move camp but they did not move. When the young men had told the news they chose six young men to go and look at the soldiers and learn who they were. The six sent out went in too far below and missed soldiers. The Cheyenne camp consisted of twenty [ca. sixty-five] lodges and six sweat lodges. The scouts of soldiers must have seen the camp and the soldiers must have kept on toward camp all during night. Daylight overtook soldiers before they reached camp. Cheyennes had eaten and sun was well up when a young man called out: "Get your guns! The soldiers are charging us!"

When Black Eagle heard this call he picked up his gun. The people all ran from the camp but he and his wife and his father-in-law remained. His father-in-law did not want to leave the camp. His lodge was on the side from which the soldiers came. The soldiers were shooting as they charged. When soldiers came to bank above the river they dismounted. (Capt. Egan's gray horse troop of 2nd Cavalry.) All were on gray horses. Black Eagle said to his wife take away your father and he started toward the soldiers. The way the bullets struck around him was like the patter of raindrops in a hard storm. He got behind a tree. He was shooting and turned the soldiers a little to one side and presently four more young men began shooting and turned them still more. He did not leave camp but the soldiers swerved off and fell in line and rode back to the main command. His wife coaxed her father to the rest of the people who had already thrown up breastworks.

The soldiers fell in line above the camp from where they had shot before and he [Black Eagle] was still behind the tree. Then he made up his mind he would be killed and started down in front of soldiers to get to river bank behind which he could hide and again the bullets pattered about him like rain but the people in the breastworks checked the soldiers. He was shooting all the time and don't know how many he killed. When she went to the breastworks the people asked her if her man was still alive and she said yes. They said go down and get him and bring him up. Presently, over all the noise of the shooting Black Eagle heard someone coming singing chief songs. He turned to look and saw a young man coming near. It was Little Creek (still living [as of 1907]). Little Creek came to him and said, "Black Eagle I have come after you. Your wife is up there and has her father there and I have come for you." There was a breastwork for the young men to fight behind, and back of that a way another breastwork for the women and children. The bank ran in a sort of amphitheatre and as the two went to the breastworks at the other end of the horse-shoe they had to show half their bodies and the bullets pattered around them like a hailstorm.

When they came to the first breastworks ten or twelve feet high he found there his wife and her father, Brave Wolf, on a horse. He was told two have been killed, a Sioux and a Cheyenne. The soldiers never stopped shooting. Little Creek was his brother-in-law. He said to Black Eagle (and the young men said the same) that he should take his three relatives—wife, father-in-law, and mother—back to big breastworks. They said we are liable to have to leave this breastwork. Black Eagle told his wife and mother to go to the breastwork behind the bank and he intended to lead his father-in-law's horse in plain sight to breastwork. It was the only way to get the horse there. When he led horse up in plain sight every soldier must have shot at him for little puffs of dust flew up all about in front of and on both sides of him. He had quite a way to go but at last he rode around the point of a hill out of sight of soldiers. When he had done so he told Brave Wolf to get off his horse. There his wife and other two women took old man back to big breastwork but he [Black Eagle] went to the ridge where all the men were.

When he went on the ridge he began to talk to the men and told them that they must work hard and not let soldiers get the women and children. Some young men spoke and said ride over that ridge. There are a lot of soldiers there in camp and herding their horses. While they were talking he said, "Some of you come with me and we will go and see where the other soldiers are." Black Eagle went over onto some high rocks where some other Cheyenne men were and looked over and saw some soldiers who were holding their horses on herd in two bunches. They went across a little valley to where a few men were holding these two bunches of horses saddled and crept up close and began to shoot at the herders and they gathered up the bunches and drove them off. (The soldiers must have been fighting on foot and have had their horses held on herd back.) Then Black Eagle and his men returned to the Cheyenne fighters. They [army herders] drove horses back to where the battle was and the soldiers all mounted and drew off and left. Soldiers captured nearly all of Indian horses and left them afoot.

After the soldiers went off, the young men all began to yell and started back to camp. In camp they found several soldiers dead and at the bank where they had been they found about three soldiers dead. The six scouts picked out came back to camp. Some young men followed up [the] command, shooting. Six scouts were mounted and took up trail following on horseback. He [Black Eagle] told them to follow them up, [saying,] "They cannot sleep with our horses to watch them." After the six scouts and four more men mounted on their only other horses had started, he started. The camp [was] all walking and women carrying what they could passed over and camped between big and little Powder Rivers. The soldiers camped on Powder River at mouth of Clear Creek and [on] same night another big command of soldiers came in and camped with them. Two big commands. The ten men waited until the middle of the night and sneaked into the camps and got together all the Indian horses and drove them off. Late in the night, Black Eagle heard someone holler: "All get up and be happy. We have recovered all our horses."

They did not reach the main body the same night. The scouts with the horses met another command of soldiers and had to sneak the horses out of sight. But on second night a young man came in and said that the horses were now getting close. When they got there each person got back his horses but they found that from three to seven of the best horses were gone out of each bunch.

Kate Bighead, Northern Cheyenne, gave her brief impressions of the Powder River battle to Thomas B. Marquis in 1927. They are excerpted from She Watched Custer's Last Battle *(Hardin, Mont.: Privately printed, 1933).*

MANY CHEYENNES, and many Sioux also, went to live in the hunting ground between the Powder and Bighorn rivers. White Bull and White Moon, my two brothers, left to go to the hunting ground, and I went with them. [Late in 1875,] word was sent to the hunting Indians that all Cheyennes and Sioux must stay on their reservations in Dakota [Territory]. But all who stayed on the reservation had their guns and ponies taken from them, so the hunters quit going there.

The band of Cheyennes where I dwelt had forty family lodges. In the last part of the winter we camped on the west side of Powder River, not far above the mouth of Little Powder river. Soldiers came early in the morning (March 17, 1876). They got between our camp and our horse herd, so all of us had to run away afoot. Not many of our people were killed, but our tepees and everything that was in them were burned. Three days later, all of us walking, we arrived at Crazy Horse's camp of Oglala Sioux.

The Oglalas gave us food and shelter. After a few days

Iron Hawk, Hunkpapa Lakota, in 1900. Courtesy of the South Dakota State Archives.

the two bands together went northward and found the Hunkpapa Sioux, where Sitting Bull was the chief. The chiefs of the three bands decided that all of us would travel together for the spring and summer hunting, as it was said that many soldiers would be coming to try to make us go back to the reservations.

Iron Hawk, a fourteen-year-old Hunkpapa Lakota, was in the Cheyenne village at the time the troops struck it. On May 12, 1907, Iron Hawk remembered the event for Judge Eli S. Ricker. The account is in the Ricker Collection, Tablet 25, Microfilm Reel 6, Nebraska State Historical Society, Lincoln.

HE WAS LIVING on Powder River with some Cheyennes and a few Oglalas. He was living on the game which they hunted. This particular time of which he speaks was in the spring when they were hunting. In the early morning— about when the sun was rising—he heard there were some soldiers surrounding them, and they began to shoot. The fighting lasted all day long, till the sun was down. The Indians left their tepees and their horses and fled on foot north to the Blue Earth, a stream at the point of it [?], and escaped. The soldiers destroyed their camp. The Indians found a vast number of other Indians camped on the Blue Earth, a small stream. These Indians in great numbers consisted of many different tribes.

Chapter 2
The Battle of Rosebud Creek, June 17, 1876
Lazy White Bull, Minneconjou Lakota; Little Hawk, Northern Cheyenne; and Young Two Moon, Northern Cheyenne

In the spring following the Cheyennes' battle with General Crook's soldiers on Powder River, the Indians converged in the Powder River–Yellowstone River region of present southeastern Montana. Aware of the army's presence, they drew together for protection and to follow age-old hunting traditions. By early June, the tribes' movement toward the Little Big Horn was underway. During the middle of that month, as General Crook once more ventured north, the warriors did an unusual thing: on June 17 they initiated an attack on Crook's column along the upper reaches of Rosebud Creek. The battle lasted for most of the day before the Lakota and Cheyenne warriors withdrew, allowing the troops to turn south once more for reinforcements. The attack prevented Crook from meeting Brigadier General Alfred H. Terry's soldiers along the Yellowstone and thereby set the stage for the Indian victory a week later on the Little Big Horn.

The Rosebud battle was fiercely contested, involving as many as fifteen hundred warriors and more than one thousand soldiers. It was fought on the high, open terrain adjoining the Rosebud and largely consisted of a series of charges and countercharges by either side in endeavoring to gain, retain, or recover the optimum high points on the field. The Sioux and Cheyennes together lost approximately eleven men killed and five wounded in the encounter; the troops listed ten men killed and twenty-one wounded.

The Indian recollections of Rosebud Creek offer examples of the individual aspects of their mode of warfare while providing insights about how these participants prepared for combat and how they viewed the battle and its meaning for their tribes.

The following account of the Rosebud battle was given by
Lazy White Bull (later Joseph White Bull) to Stanley Vestal
(Walter Stanley Campbell) about 1930. Lazy White Bull (1850–
1947), a Minneconjou Lakota, was a nephew of Sitting Bull, the
famous Hunkpapa leader who was prominent throughout the
events of 1876. His recollections are excerpted from Vestal,
Warpath: The True Story of the Fighting Sioux Told in a Biography of Chief Joseph White Bull *(Boston: Houghton Mifflin*
Company, 1934).

DURING MAY AND JUNE, Sitting Bull's great camp was
hunting on the Rosebud and the Little Big Horn, and all
this time Sitting Bull kept scouts out. But for a long time
they had nothing to report. By the middle of June, the
game and the grazing on the Rosebud had become exhausted and the camps were moving back to the Little Big
Horn looking for buffalo. On the evening of June 16, the
tipis were pitched on Reno (Ash) Creek, between the
Rosebud and the Little Big Horn. That night, Cheyenne
scouts came in and reported the valley of the Rosebud
black with soldiers. General George "Three Stars" Crook
was coming from Fort Fetterman, Wyoming, with more
than a thousand white soldiers and two hundred and sixty
Indian Scouts—Crows, Shoshoni, Rees [Arikaras]—a force
of more than thirteen hundred men.

Makes-Room was attending a meeting in the Cheyenne camp when the scouts came in. He hurried back to
his own camp circle and spread the news. All the Sioux
began to prepare for battle. They expected a hard fight.

White Bull put on a pair of dark blue woolen leggins
decorated with broad stripes of blue-and-white beads, and
beaded moccasins to match. Before and behind he hung a
long red flannel breech-cloth reaching to his ankles,
tucked under his belt over his regular loin-cloth. He put
on a shirt, and over his right shoulder he hung the thong
which supported the small rawhide hoop, to which was

attached four small leather pouches of medicine (earth of different kinds), a buffalo tail, and an eagle feather. This was his war-charm. It hung under his left arm. Around his waist, like a kilt, he placed his folded black blanket and belted it there with his cartridge-belt containing a hundred cartridges. He borrowed a fine war-bonnet from his brother-in-law, Bad Lake.

This bonnet had a long tail of eagle feathers reaching to the ground. The feathers began at the crown of the head and went straight down the back. There were no feathers around the head on this bonnet. All the way down the tail this bonnet was colored red and white alternately—seven white feathers, then four red, and so on. These red feathers commemorated wounds received in battle. A man who wore such red feathers dared not tell a lie or he might be wounded.

This bonnet had no protective power: White Bull wore it for its beauty. If he were to be killed, he wished to die in these fine war-clothes. Otherwise those who saw him lying on the battlefield might say: "This was a poor man. He must not have been a good warrior. See how shabby he lies there." Besides, such fine war-clothes made a man more courageous.

White Bull took his seventeen-shot repeating rifle, which he had purchased from an Agency Indian at Fort Bennett [along the Missouri River in Dakota Territory]. Then he went out and saddled a fast horse. He tied an eagle feather in its forelock and tail and fastened an imitation scalp made of woman's hair to his bridle-bit. Only horses which had been used to ride down an enemy could wear such a decoration. Then White Bull rode over to [his uncle] Sitting Bull's tent where the warriors were gathered.

Almost a thousand warriors had assembled—Cheyenne, Oglala, Minniconjou, Sans Arc, Brulé, Hunkpapa. It was late at night when they set out. They rode until nearly daybreak, then stopped, unsaddled, and let their

Lazy White Bull, Minneconjou Lakota, 1880s. Photograph by George W. Scott. Courtesy of the State Historical Society of North Dakota.

horses rest. At daybreak they saddled up and rode on until they came near a big hill. There they halted again and sent scouts forward to the top of this hill to look for the troops. When these scouts had traveled halfway to the hilltop,

Indian Government scouts appeared there, and firing was heard.

The whole war-party whipped up their horses and charged for the hill. There they found a Sioux wounded, and a horse killed. They rode over the hill and saw five Government scouts dashing downhill to the troops. They charged these five men, shooting all the time, and wounded one of them. Still they pressed on, following the five scouts, close to the soldiers.

The soldiers advanced, firing at the Indians. A Cheyenne had his horse shot under him. The Sioux who rode with him were all surrounded and killed. They got caught between two bodies of enemies. It was a hard fight.

White Bull was not much given to singing war-songs, but as he advanced into that fight he was inspired to sing a song composed on the spot:

> Friends, try your best.
> I do not wish my father to be made ashamed.
> Because he is a chief.

There was a brave Cheyenne wearing a war-bonnet and red leggins who led the attack. White Bull kept trying to get in front of this brave man, but could not; the Cheyenne had the better horse. But as the Government scouts and the soldiers came charging back, White Bull stood his ground and the Cheyenne retreated past him. White Bull was out in front at last. The enemies kept coming, and in the lead dashed a brave Shoshoni [army scout]. He was riding a fast bald-faced sorrel with white stockings. His horse's tail was tied up in red flannel and a red flannel strip was tied about its neck. This Shoshoni had a cartridge-belt and a repeating rifle. He came straight for White Bull.

On came the Shoshoni, and White Bull sped to meet him. When he came near, the Shoshoni fired twice — but missed. White Bull pumped two bullets into the right foreshoulder of the sorrel horse and dropped it. He ran the Shoshoni down and lamed him in the right leg, then wheeled away to join his comrades in retreat.

Afterward White Bull learned from the Crows that this Shoshoni was one of the bravest of their warriors. This Shoshoni was still living a few years ago: he may be alive today. This was considered one of the bravest of White Bull's many deeds, and, when President Coolidge visited the Black Hills and White Bull was chosen to make the address of welcome for the Indians, the Chief was pointed out as The-Man-Who-Lamed-the-Shoshoni.

It may be interesting to know White Bull's opinion of the various enemies he fought with: Says he: "The Rees are good fighters. The Flatheads fight well on foot with guns, but if you once get them to running, they sure do run. The Crows and the white soldiers are about the same at long-range shooting, but in hand-to-hand combat the Crows are more dangerous. But of all the enemies I have fought, the Shoshoni are the bravest and best warriors."

It was back and forth that day. All day long the Indians of both sides charged back and forth [on] horseback and not a few were killed on both sides. The troops lost nine men killed and twenty-one wounded. Of White Bull's immediate friends, Little Crow, Black Bird, Sitting Bear, and Little Wolf perished.

There were many thrilling rescues. White Bull's brother, One Bull, saved Yells-at-Daybreak (His-Voice-is Loudest-at-Daybreak, sometimes translated Rooster). White Bull himself saved Hawk Soldier after he was shot from his horse. He carried him back to his uncle. In another part of the fight a horse was shot and the Indian rider was pinned down. His leg was caught under the dead horse. White Bull ran forward and protected him until he could get his foot free and escape.

There was a Cheyenne in this fight named Sunrise.

He was painted yellow all over and wore a stuffed water-dog [salamander] tied in his hair for a war-charm. He was shot through the belly from behind and lay helpless. White Bull dismounted and ran forward under fire. He seized the Cheyenne by the wrists and dragged him back to safety. The Cheyennes still honor White Bull for saving this man. Sunrise died after they got him back to camp. Because of his war-charm some of the Sioux remember him as Water-Dog.

This was one of the hardest fights White Bull ever saw. It lasted all day, but when it was over "Three Stars" took his troops and hit the trail back to his base. The Sioux and Cheyennes rode home, leaving scouts behind to watch "Three Stars" movements.

Two days later the Sioux returned to the battlefield. They found the body of a government scout there. Some say the Indians dug up the bodies of the white soldiers buried there, but White Bull knows nothing of this.

There is one strange thing about the Three Stars' battle. A certain Cheyenne rode into the fight, singing:

I do not wish to be an old man.
This day is mine to die.

That Cheyenne was killed in the fight. White Bull is puzzled to know how the Cheyenne knew he was to die that day. He says he never saw an Indian throw his life away deliberately in battle or commit suicide in a fight.

The Northern Cheyenne warrior, Little Hawk, was twenty-eight years old at the time of the Rosebud Creek battle. He furnished his reminiscences to George Bird Grinnell on September 5, 1908. They are in Notebook 348, Grinnell Collection, Braun Research Library, Southwest Museum, Los Angeles.

THEY [THE CHEYENNES] were camped down at big bend of Rosebud when he went to Brave Wolf and proposed that

Little Hawk, Northern Cheyenne, 1880s. Courtesy of the Nebraska State Historical Society.

they should go to war. When they set out they came south from big bend through this country and went over on Pole Creek. As they were about to go down into the valley they discovered a lot of soldiers coming but soldiers did not see them. They turned about and came back. They came down Rosebud and found Cheyenne camp at mouth of Muddy. They reported soldiers on Pole Creek. A good many young men who were brave and strong and able to make a quick trip . . . started after night and travelled all next day going a little way and then stopping. Scouts sent ahead had discovered that soldiers had come as far as Tongue River and had stopped there. They went close to Tongue River and waited, having determined to make a night charge thinking that they could stampede the soldier horses. When night came and they thought soldiers were sleeping, they slipped up close and charged and began to shoot but the soldiers must have been sitting up with guns in their hands for a rain of bullets met them. They fought for a time but no one was killed on either side, so far as they knew. Then they left soldiers and came away and returned to their camp.[2] This was in 1876.

When camp moved they went to where . . . [Thompson Creek] now is and then to Reno Creek. That night Little Hawk called four young men, and said to them let us go out and see if we can not get some horses from the white people. They saddled up and started. They went through the Wolf Mountains then went on, at length stopped to wait for day. At day they went on and struck through the hills and about noon reached the big bend of Rosebud. . . . As they went down Rosebud they saw a big herd of [buffalo] bulls. Little Hawk told the young men that they would kill one and would roast some meat. He approached the bulls and shot one, and broke its back and it dragged itself down near the creek and they killed it and found close to it a nice spring. They began to skin the buffalo and one started a fire.

Before they had the meat roasted a big band of buffalo cows came in sight. They told Crooked Nose to stay and roast the meat while they went to look for a fatter animal. The men were Yellow Eagle . . . [,] Crooked Nose . . . [,] Little Shield . . . [,] White Bird . . . [and] Little Hawk. . . . They looked back at Crooked Nose cooking meat and saw that he was motioning them from side to side for them to come back. They turned their horses and rode back without killing this fat cow. When they reached him, Crooked Nose said to them, "On that hill by those red buttes I saw two men looking over and after looking a little while they rode up in sight, each leading a horse. They rode out of sight toward us. I think they are coming in our direction right toward us." Little Hawk said, "Saddle up quick. I think those are Sioux. We will have some fun with them."

They saddled and rode up a little gulch. When they got up there a little way he [Little Hawk] stopped his horse and looked over and as he raised his head it seemed as if the whole earth were black with soldiers. He said to his friends, "They are soldiers," but he said it very low for the soldiers were so close that he was afraid they would hear him. He turned and got on his horse and Little Shield said, "The best thing we can do is to go back to where we were roasting meat. There is timber on the creek and there we can make a stand." But Little Hawk did not hear him say this and jumped on his horse and started and the others followed him. As he was riding, he lost his field glasses but he did not stop. He went down to Rosebud and into the brush and through it up the creek. He left a good many locks of his hair in the brush.

Keeping on up the Rosebud and so out of sight of troops who had not yet reached the river, they came to a big high butte about three miles above soldiers. They were not discovered. There they stopped and looked back. They could still see the soldiers coming down the hill with the naked eye. If they had not killed the buffalo they would have kept on and ridden right into the soldiers. The buffalo bull saved their lives. Coming up the creek they did not lope. They just raced their horses fast as they could go.

When they left this round butte they rode on over the mountains toward the Little Big Horn. After they had crossed the mountains they rode along the foothills of the Wolf Mountains and just as day began to break they came to the camp which had moved just a little way down Reno Creek. When they got near camp they began to howl like wolves to notify them that something had been seen. Some early rising Sioux came out and met them and asked, "Who are you, Sioux or Cheyenne?" They said, "Cheyenne," and the Sioux turned and left them but notified the Cheyennes that some of their people were coming. Soon the whole camp was aroused. They got into camp just at good daylight. They supposed this was the big outfit of which Custer's command was a part.[3] When they reached camp all the men began to catch their horses and to get ready. All painted themselves, put on their war bonnets, paraded about the camp two-by-two, and then struck out for the soldiers going straight through the hills.

About midday they reached the place where the soldiers were camped, just where they had first seen them. Many people charged, but one man who had the best horse was in the lead. [This was] Chief Comes In Sight. His horse's hind leg was broken before he reached the soldiers. The Cheyennes retreated toward the hills and left Chief Comes In Sight on foot. He was walking away and all the soldiers were shooting at him as hard as they could. His sister was with the party riding a gray horse. She looked down and saw her brother there and rushed down to meet her brother and he jumped behind her and she brought him off. Neither was hit. The soldiers made a charge and drove the Cheyennes back, but the Cheyennes charged, White Shield leading, and drove the soldiers.

They came near killing a whole company. They fought till late in evening and then stopped. Only one Cheyenne was killed in fight, . . . Thin Hair. He was shot through the bowels from in front backward.

Young Two Moon (John Two Moon) was the nephew of Chief Two Moon of the Northern Cheyennes. Born in 1855, Young Two Moon was twenty-one years old when his people fought Crook. His account of the Rosebud Battle was given to George Bird Grinnell on September 12, 1908. It is in Notebook 348, George Bird Grinnell Collection, Braun Research Library, Southwest Museum, Los Angeles.

THE MAN WHO BROUGHT news into camp was Little Hawk. Camp was on Reno Creek. With some of the others he [Young Two Moon] rode about camp watching and listening—as if guards. Before anyone had come in, they were expecting something to happen and thought that they would be the first ones out. The first thing they heard was some one coming howling like a wolf. When they heard this they knew that someone was coming who had seen something. As soon as he heard it he rode toward the sound. When they reached Little Hawk, one of them asked, "What is it?" Little Hawk said, "Pretty near to the head of Rosebud where it bends to turn into the hills, as we were roasting meat we saw soldiers—I think there are many Indians with them too. They may come right down the Rosebud." As soon as they could get ready, all the young men set out. John Two Moon came on with a party that struck Rosebud about the mouth of Thompson Creek. They got about two miles above this. They were headed off by the Cheyenne soldiers, who formed a line and would let them go no farther, because Little Hawk had expressed the opinion that the white soldiers were coming down the stream. They did not know where Little Hawk was but he had led a large party across through the Wolf Mountains.

There were about 200 men with Two Moon's party and one woman. They sent on ahead two Sioux and two Cheyennes. They were told if they found the troops to come back at once. After these four had been gone for some time the main body started after them.

Four Indians had been sent out for the troops as scouts on the east side of Rosebud. The four scouts sent out by Sioux and Cheyennes and those for the white troops saw each other. Scouts for troops were on the ridge but the four men for the Cheyennes and Sioux were down in the bottom. The four turned about. The scouts of the white soldiers turned about and rode back to the command. The Sioux and Cheyenne scouts rode zigzag as a sign that they had seen something and all the Indians in line down the creek charged up toward them. Before they came in sight of the soldiers this party could hear the guns and knew that they were fighting and kept on up the stream. Soon they heard the guns to the right and, leaving the bottom, crossed over the hills to the river again. They reached the top of the hills looking down into the Rosebud Valley and could see the soldiers chasing the Indians back into the hills. The soldiers were pretty strong. They could see the horses of the Indians falling and being wounded as they climbed the hills. They did not stop long on the divide but charged down on the soldiers, who stopped their pursuit and fell back.

Now the party with Little Hawk turned their horses and charged so that there was a big body of men charging down on the soldiers. Chief Comes In Sight's sister charged down with the men. On the side from which they charged there was a little ridge running down and when they reached this Indians all dismounted and it hid them. Beyond was a nice level piece of ground. The Indians did not stay there. They mounted and started down toward the hills. Those who were out on the level ground, they had to fight though there was little cover. After Indians got back out of sight again Two Moon looked over and saw four cavalry horses starting toward the hill. Two Moon and Black Coyote started down after them and behind them two Cheyennes [and] two Sioux started. When they came in sight charging down, the soldiers made a charge to drive them back. Soldiers came near overtaking them and were shooting at them fast. Then Two Moon went too far to one side and did not get the horses. The soldiers charged him and he went a little too far so that the soldiers almost caught them. Then they turned back.

There was now fighting all along the line. The company of soldiers which were charging straight down stopped near the river. The six men who had charged when they saw they could do nothing, turned and went to join another body of Indians that were coming in above them. This body was chiefly of Cheyennes. They did not later go into the fight. Two men here did brave things. White Shield and a Sioux. They made a charge on the troops and Indians followed. When charge began the troops were dismounted, but when the charge was made they all mounted and retreated towards the main body of troops. The soldiers did not run far but wheeled and fell in line and fired a volley and then mounted and ran. Here White Shield killed a man, counted coup on and ran over him. The Sioux did the same.

On top of a little ridge the soldiers dismounted again. They tried to hold back Indians but after an officer was shot the body of Indians coming against them was great and troops retreated. Here a soldier could not mount his horse and White Shield rode between him and his horse to knock the reins out of his hand and free them. He killed and counted coup on this man who had a bugle. When Indians left the ridge from which troops had been driven they had to cross a steep gulch to get upon the next flat. On the flat a white soldier fell off or was wounded and lost his horse. A Cheyenne named Scabby Island [Eyelid?] rode up to the soldier and tried to strike him with his whip. The soldier caught whip and pulled Indian off his horse. This soldier and this Indian got away unhurt.

The [army] Indian scouts . . . now made a charge and Sioux and Cheyennes ran. They now retreated across the deep gulch just crossed before. After crossing this the Cheyennes and Sioux wheeled and fired once and then turned and ran again. The number of soldiers was great. Now the soldiers made a strong charge and then Indians divided, some going down the ridge and some up. Two Moon left the ridge and when he got on the flat his horse got out of wind and there were the soldiers close behind him and coming fast. The Cheyennes who were up above could see a person there alone whose horse had given out.

Two Moon thought that this was his last day. He had to dismount, leave his horse and run off on foot. The bullets were flying pretty thick and were knocking up the dirt all about him. He saw before him a man advancing on a buckskin horse and he thought he was going to have some help, but the bullets flew so thick that the man turned and rode away. Again he saw a man coming toward him riding a spotted horse. He recognized the person, Young Black Bird (now White Shield). White Shield ran up to his side and told Two Moon to jump on behind him and he did so. So White Shield saved his life that day. They did not go very far, but farther than he could have gone afoot, when that horse began to lose its wind and give out. Soon they saw another man coming leading a horse that he had captured from the Indian scouts of the troops. It was Contrary Belly. Meantime two Sioux had dashed up to the two men but when they got close one of them said they are Cheyennes and they rode away. Then Contrary Belly came up and Two Moon jumped on the led horse and rode away. When they reached the main body of Sioux and Cheyennes they stopped and made a stand. The soldiers were still coming but there were so many Indians they stood them off. Here the fight stopped. The Cheyennes and Sioux stayed there a little while and then went away and left soldiers. Many men were wounded and many horses killed and wounded so that many Indians were on foot. After this fight Young Blackbird's name was changed to White Shield.

Chapter 3
The Battle of
the Little Big Horn,
June 25–26, 1876

*Red Horse, Minneconjou Lakota; She Walks with Her
Shawl, Hunkpapa Lakota; Brave Wolf, Northern
Cheyenne; American Horse, Oglala Lakota; Soldier Wolf,
Northern Cheyenne; Tall Bull, Northern Cheyenne;
One Bull, Minneconjou Lakota; Flying By, Minneconjou
Lakota; Little Hawk, Northern Cheyenne; White Bull,
Northern Cheyenne; and Young Two Moon,
Northern Cheyenne*

*The tribes that gathered in the Little Big Horn Valley by June 25,
1876, composed the largest known gathering of Indians ever to
occur on the northern plains. They represented all the Lakota
tribes—Hunkpapas, Oglalas, Minneconjous, Brulés, Blackfeet,
Two Kettles, and Sans Arcs, besides members of diverse eastern
Sioux groups and the Northern Cheyennes. Inspired by such
leaders as Sitting Bull, Crazy Horse, Gall, Crow King, Lame
White Man, and Two Moon, the Indians, whose encampment
swelled to as many as eight thousand people, including upwards
of twenty-five hundred warriors, anticipated the presence of the
soldiers, whose approach their scouts had monitored.*

*In composition, the assemblage included the so-called
Northern Sioux, those people who had spurned all attempts by
the U.S. government to bring them within the bounds of the
Great Sioux Reservation established in 1868. Besides the securi-
ty-concious Cheyennes, perhaps its most numerous components
derived from the Sioux agencies themselves—people who had
departed the reservation to join their nonagency kin for summer
hunting and ritual ceremonial activities.*

*Having fought Crook's soldiers at Rosebud Creek, many of
the warriors in the Little Big Horn encampment were falsely*

31

confident that the army would not further molest them. Thus, the attack of Lieutenant Colonel George A. Custer's Seventh Cavalry at midday on June 25 seems to have caught the tribesmen largely unaware. But they responded well. The Battle of the Little Big Horn took the form of two major actions. The first, wherein an army battalion under Major Marcus A. Reno charged the south end of the village, ended with the warriors' driving these troops from the valley after they had endured substantial losses. Although Reno gained the bluff tops east of the river and was joined by reinforcements, the Indians succeeded in isolating the soldiers over the next two days. The second action involved the precipitate defeat and death of Custer's immediate command on rugged terrain nearly four miles north of Reno's action.

The overwhelming nature of the warriors' victory over Custer's soldiers in time produced one of the salient image-evoking events in American history. Because of the mystery among whites regarding Custer's course to defeat, Indian accounts were initially sought out for purposes of explanation. This participant testimony was largely dismissed as irreconcilable, owing mostly to failures in translation (often compounded by the sensational coverage of newspaper correspondents) coupled with genuine fears of retribution among the Sioux and Cheyenne people. Eventually, however, Indian accounts of Little Big Horn gained in credibility as more objective interviewers became involved. As a result, Indian accounts of their victory on the Greasy Grass today constitute an authoritative body of data that has enriched knowledge of that event.

The following accounts of Little Big Horn offer the perspectives of five Lakotas (including one woman) and six Northern Cheyennes. Individual in nature, the accounts nonetheless share similarities that enhance the significance of such testimony in explaining the intertribal defeat of the soldiers in 1876.

In 1881 the forty-six-year-old Minneconjou chief, Red Horse, contributed one of the earliest Indian reminiscences of the Battle of the Little Big Horn to Dr. Charles E. McChesney, an acting assistant surgeon, U.S. Army. Red Horse accompanied his recollections with forty-one pictograph drawings, only four of which are presented here. The Minneconjou's account is drawn from Tenth Annual Report of the Bureau of Ethnology (Washington, D.C.: Government Printing Office,

1893), which reproduced ten of the Red Horse drawings. Bracketed material is as it appears in the original publication, except for that preceded by an asterisk, which has been inserted into this generation.

FIVE SPRINGS AGO I, with many Sioux Indians, took down and packed up our tipis and moved from Cheyenne river to the Rosebud river, where we camped a few days; then took down and packed up our lodges and moved to the Little Bighorn river and pitched our lodges with the large camp of Sioux.

The Sioux were camped on the Little Bighorn river as follows: The lodges of the Uncpapas were pitched highest up the river under a bluff. The Santee lodges were pitched next. The Oglala's [*sic] lodges were pitched next. The Brulé lodges were pitched next. The Minneconjou lodges were pitched next. The Sans Arcs' lodges were pitched next. The Blackfeet lodges were pitched next. The Cheyenne lodges were pitched next. A few Arikara [*Arapaho?] Indians were among the Sioux (being without lodges of their own.

I was a Sioux chief in the council lodge. My lodge was pitched in the center of the camp. The day of the attack I and four women were a short distance from the camp digging wild turnips. Suddenly one of the women attracted my attention to a cloud of dust rising a short distance from camp. I soon saw that the soldiers were charging the camp. To the camp I and the women ran. When I arrived a person told me to hurry to the council lodge. The soldiers charged so quickly we could not talk (council). We came out of the council lodge and talked in all directions. The Sioux mount horses, take guns, and go fight the soldiers. Women and children mount horses and go, meaning to get out of the way.

Among the soldiers was an officer who rode a horse with four white feet. [From Dr. McChesney's memoranda

Red Horse, Minneconjou Lakota. Photograph by David F. Barry. Courtesy of the State Historical Society of North Dakota.

this officer was Capt. French, Seventh Cavalry.] The Sioux have for a long time fought many brave men of different people, but the Sioux say this officer was the bravest man

they had ever fought. I don't know whether this was Gen.
Custer or not. Many of the Sioux men that I hear talking
tell me it was. I saw this officer in the fight many times, but
did not see his body. It has been told me that he was killed
by a Santee Indian, who took his horse. This officer wore a
large-brimmed hat and a deerskin coat. This officer saved
the lives of many soldiers by turning his horse and cover-
ing the retreat. Sioux say this officer was the bravest man
they ever fought. I saw two officers looking alike, both
having long yellowish hair.

Before the attack the Sioux were camped on the
Rosebud river. Sioux moved down a river running into the
Little Bighorn river, crossed the Little Bighorn river, and
camped on its west bank.

This day [day of attack] a Sioux man started to go to
Red Cloud agency, but when he had gone a short distance
from camp he saw a cloud of dust rising and turned back
and said he thought a herd of buffalo was coming near the
village.

The day was hot. In a short time the soldiers charged
the camp. [This was Maj. Reno's battalion of the Seventh
Cavalry.] The soldiers came on the trail made by the Sioux
camp in moving, and crossed the Little Bighorn river
above where the women and children ran down the Little
Bighorn river a short distance into a ravine. The soldiers
set fire to the lodges. All the Sioux now charged the
soldiers and drove them in confusion across the Little
Bighorn river, which was very rapid, and several soldiers
were drowned in it. On a hill the soldiers stopped and the
Sioux surrounded them. A Sioux man came and said that a
different party went around, and the Sioux all heard it and
left the soldiers on the hill and went quickly to save the
women and children.

From the hill that the soldiers were on to the place
where the different soldiers [by this term Red-Horse
always means the battalion immediately commanded by

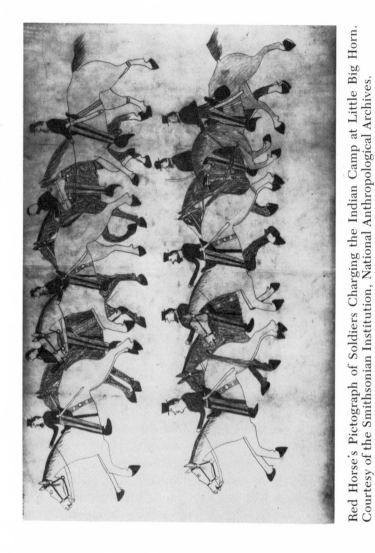

Red Horse's Pictograph of Soldiers Charging the Indian Camp at Little Big Horn. Courtesy of the Smithsonian Institution, National Anthropological Archives.

General Custer, his mode of distinction being that they were a different body from that first encountered] were seen was level ground with the exception of a creek. Sioux thought the soldiers on the hill [i.e., Reno's battalion] would charge them in rear, but when they did not the Sioux throught the soldiers on the hill were out of cartridges. As soon as we had killed all the different soldiers, the Sioux all went back to kill the soldiers on the hill. All the Sioux watched around the hill on which were the soldiers until a Sioux man came and said many walking soldiers were coming near. The coming of the walking soldiers was the saving of the soldiers on the hill. Sioux can not fight the walking soldiers [infantry], being afraid of them, so the Sioux hurriedly left.

The soldiers charged the Sioux camp about noon. The soldiers were divided, one party charging right into the camp. After driving these soldiers across the river, the Sioux charged the different soldiers [i.e., Custer's] below, and drove them in confusion; these soldiers became foolish, many throwing away their guns and raising their hands, saying, "Sioux, pity us; take us prisoners." The Sioux did not take a single soldier prisoner, but killed all of them; none were left alive for even a few minutes. Those different soldiers discharged their guns but little. I took a gun and two belts off two dead soldiers; out of one belt two cartridges were gone, out of the other five.

The Sioux took the guns and cartridges off the dead soldiers and went to the hill on which the soldiers were, surrounded and fought them with the guns and cartridges of the dead soldiers. Had the soldiers not divided I think they would have killed many Sioux. The different soldiers [i.e., Custer's battalion] that the Sioux killed made five brave stands. Once the Sioux charged right in the midst of the different soldiers and scattered them all, fighting among the soldiers hand to hand.

Red Horse's Pictograph of the Sioux Fighting Custer's Battalion. Courtesy of the Smithsonian Institution, National Anthropological Archives.

Red Horse's Pictograph of the Dead Sioux. Courtesy of the Smithsonian Institution, National Anthropological Archives.

One band of soldiers was in rear of the Sioux. When this band of soldiers charged, the Sioux fell back, and the Sioux and the soldiers stood facing each other. Then all the Sioux became brave and charged the soldiers. The Sioux went but a short distance before they separated and surrounded the soldiers. I could see the officers riding in front of the soldiers and hear them shouting. Now the Sioux had many killed. The soldiers killed 136 and wounded 160 Sioux.[4] The Sioux killed all these different soldiers in the ravine.

The soldiers [*under Reno initially] charged the Sioux camp farthest up the river. A short time after, the different soldiers [*Custer's] charged the village below. While the different soldiers and Sioux were fighting together the Sioux chief said, "Sioux men, go watch the soldiers on the hill and prevent their joining the different soldiers." The Sioux men took the clothing off the dead and dressed themselves in it. Among the soldiers were white men who were not [*dressed as?] soldiers. The Sioux dressed in the soldiers' and white men's clothing fought the soldiers on the hill.

The banks of the Little Bighorn river were high and the Sioux killed many of the soldiers while crossing [*during Reno's retreat]. The soldiers on the hill dug up the ground [i.e., made earthworks], and the soldiers and Sioux fought at long range, sometimes the Sioux charging close up. The fight continued at long range until a Sioux man saw the walking soldiers coming. When the walking soldiers came near, the Sioux became afraid and ran away.

The following woman's account of the battle was given by She Walks with Her Shawl, Hunkpapa Lakota, to Walter S. Campbell (Stanley Vestal) in 1931. It is Item 5e, Box 111, in the Walter S. Campbell Collection, Division of Manuscripts, Western History Collections, University of Oklahoma Libraries, Norman.

Red Horse's Pictograph of Custer's Dead Cavalry. Courtesy of the Smithsonian Institution, National Anthropological Archives.

I WAS BORN SEVENTY-SEVEN WINTERS AGO, near Grand
River, [in present] South Dakota. My father, Slohan, was
the bravest man among our people. Fifty-five years ago we
packed our tents and went with other Indians to Peji-sla-
wakpa (Greasy Grass). We were then living on the Standing Rock Indian reservation [Great Sioux Reservation,
Standing Rock Agency]. I belonged to Sitting Bull's band.
They were great fighters. We called ourselves Hunkpapa.
This means confederated bands. When I was still a young
girl (about seventeen) I accompanied a Sioux war party
which made war against the Crow Indians in Montana. My
father went to war 70 times. He was wounded nearly a
dozen times.

But I am going to tell you of the greatest battle. This
was a fight against Pehin-hanska (General Custer). I was
several miles from the Hunkpapa camp when I saw a cloud
of dust rise beyond a ridge of bluffs in the east. The
morning was hot and sultry. Several of us Indian girls were
digging wild turnips. I was then 23 years old. We girls
looked towards the camp and saw a warrior ride swiftly,
shouting that the soldiers were only a few miles away and
that the women and children including old men should run
for the hills in an opposite direction.

I dropped the pointed ash stick which I had used in
digging turnips and rans towards my tipi. I saw my father
running towards the horses. When I got to my tent,
mother told me that news was brought to her that my
brother had been killed by the soldiers. My brother had
gone early that morning in search for a horse that strayed
from our herd. In a few moments we saw soldiers on
horseback on a bluff just across the Greasy Grass (Little
Big Horn) river. I knew that there would be a battle
because I saw warriors getting their horses and tomahawks.

I heard Hawkman shout, Ho-ka-he! Ho-ka-he!
(Charge.) The soldiers began firing into our camp. Then

they ceased firing. I saw my father preparing to go to battle. I sang a death song for my brother who had been killed.

My heart was bad. Revenge! Revenge! For my brother's death. I thought of the death of my young brother, One Hawk. Brown Eagle, my brother's companion on that morning had escaped and gave the alarm to the camp that the soldiers were coming. I ran to a nearby thicket and got my black horse. I painted my face with crimson and unbraided my black hair. I was mourning. I was a woman, but I was not afraid.

By this time the soldiers (Reno's men) were forming a battle line in the bottom about a half mile away. In another moment I heard a terrific volley of carbines. The bullets shattered the tipi poles. Women and children were running away from the gunfire. In the tumult I heard old men and women singing death songs for their warriors who were now ready to attack the soldiers. The chanting of death songs made me brave, although I was a woman. I saw a warrior adjusting his quiver and grasping his tomahawk. He started running towards his horse when he suddenly recoiled and dropped dead. He was killed near his tipi.

Warriors were given orders by Hawkman to mount their horses and follow the fringe of a forest and wait until commands were given to charge. The soldiers kept on firing. Some women were also killed. Horses and dogs too! The camp was in great commotion.

Father led my black horse up to me and I mounted. We galloped towards the soldiers. Other warriors joined in with us. When we were nearing the fringe of the woods an order was given by Hawkman to charge. Ho-ka-he! Ho-ka-he! Charge! Charge! The warriors were now near the soldiers. The troopers were all on foot. They shot straight, because I saw our leader killed as he rode with his warriors.

The charge was so stubborn that the soldiers ran to their horses and, mounting them, rode swiftly towards the

Gall, Hunkpapa Lakota leader. Photograph by David F. Barry, 1880. Courtesy of the National Archives (photo no. 111-sc-82572).

river. The Greasy Grass river was very deep. Their horses had to swim to get across. Some of the warriors rode into the water and tomahawked the soldiers. In the charge the Indians rode among the troopers and with tomahawks unhorsed several of them. The soldiers were very excited. Some of them shot into the air. The Indians chased the soldiers across the river and up over a bluff.

Then the warriors returned to the bottom where the first battle took place. We heard a commotion far down the valley. The warriors rode in a column of fives. They sang a victory song. Someone said that another body of soldiers were attacking the lower end of the village. I heard afterwards that the soldiers were under the command of Long Hair (Custer). With my father and other youthful warriors I rode in that direction.

We crossed the Greasy Grass below a beaver dam (the water is not so deep there) and came upon many horses. One soldier was holding the reins of eight or ten horses. An Indian waved his blanket and scared all the horses. They got away from the men (troopers). On the ridge just north of us I saw blue-clad men running up a ravine, firing as they ran.

The dust created from the stampeding horses and powder smoke made everything dark and black. Flashes from carbines could be seen. The valley was dense with powder smoke. I never heard such whooping and shouting. "There was never a better day to die," shouted Red Horse. In the battle I heard cries from troopers, but could not understand what they were saying. I do not speak English.

Long Hair's troopers were trapped in an enclosure. There were Indians everywhere. The Cheyennes attacked the soldiers from the north and Crow King from the South. The Sioux Indians encircled the troopers. Not one got away! The Sioux used tomahawks. It was not a massacre, but [a] hotly contested battle between two armed forces. Very few soldiers were mutilated, as oft has been said by the whites. Not a single soldier was burned at the stake. Sioux Indians do not torture their victims.

After the battle the Indians took all the equipment

and horses belonging to the soldiers. The brave men who came to punish us that morning were defeated; but in the end, the Indians lost. We saw the body of Long Hair. Of course, we did not know who the soldiers were until an interpreter told us that the men came from Fort Lincoln, then [in] Dakota Territory. On the saddle blankets were the cross saber insignia and the letter seven.

The victorious warriors returned to the camp, as did the women and children who could see the battle from where they took refuge. Over sixty Indians were killed and they were also brought back to the camp for scaffold-burial. The Indians did not stage a victory dance that night. They were mourning for their own dead. . . .

The Northern Cheyenne Brave Wolf recalled the Little Big Horn in an interview with George Bird Grinnell in 1895. The account is in Item 497, "Notes on the Custer Fight," Grinnell Collection, Braun Research Library, Southwest Museum, Los Angeles.

I WAS IN THE CHEYENNE CAMP and when Reno made his charge I went with the rest to meet him. We fought there. I saw the soldiers all go down the timber, they fought there for a little while and then they all ran out of the timber. I could never understand why they left it, if they had stayed there, they would have been all right, but they ran out of the timber and across the river and up the hill. The citizen packers and the pack mules were on the hill before Reno got there,[5] then we heard the shooting below, and all rushed down the river. When I got to the Cheyenne camp, the fighting had been going on for some time. The soldiers (Custer's), were right down close to the stream, but none were on this [west] side. Just as I got there, the soldiers began to retreat up the narrow gulch. They were all drawn up in line of battle, shooting well and fighting hard, but there were so many people around them, that they could not help being killed. They still held their line of battle and

Brave Wolf, Northern Cheyenne, early 1900s. Photograph by
Elizabeth C. Grinnell. Courtesy of the Southwest Museum.
Photo no. N.41033 P.10713.

kept fighting and falling from their horses; fighting and
falling all the way up, nearly to where the monument now
stands. I think all their horses had been killed before they

got quite to the top of the hill. None got there on horseback, and only a few on foot. A part of those who had
reached the top of the hill, went on over and tried to go to
the stream, but they killed them all going down the hill,
before any of them got to the creek. It was hard fighting,
very hard all the time. I have been in many hard fights, but
I never saw such brave men.

*American Horse provided reminiscences to Grinnell in 1895.
The Oglala Lakota became a prominent orator and negotiator
among his people in the days preceding and following the
Wounded Knee crisis in 1890. His account of the Little Big Horn
is in the Grinnell Collection, Item 497, "Notes on the Custer
Fight," Braun Research Library, Southwest Museum, Los Angeles.*

WE FIRST CAME TOGETHER and heard that the white
soldiers were in the country, down near the mouth of the
Rosebud close to the Yellowstone; a large camp gathered
there. After a time we all moved up the Rosebud, keeping
scouts out all the time. While we were going up the
Rosebud, we had a fight with the soldiers [of General
Crook]. Afterward we crossed over to Reno Creek and
camped; then scouts came in and said that lots of white
men (soldiers) were coming.

Next morning we moved on and camped in a big
bottom where there is a bunch of timber, the place where
we were afterwards attacked [at the Little Big Horn].
Scouts were kept out all the time. The next day some men
were back on the Rosebud watching to see where the
troops with whom they had fought, were going. These
went the other way, but these scouts discovered Custer
going up the Rosebud. A short time after the scout who
made this discovery got into the camp, four or five lodges
of Sioux who had set out to go to Red Cloud Agency
discovered Custer's troops close to them. These lodges got

frightened and turned back, and when they reached the main camp, their report caused great alarm.

Above, where the Indians had left the Rosebud, two men wounded in the first fight on the Rosebud had died and been left there in lodges. The troops discovered these lodges, and charged them and found no one there alive. The scouts of the Indians saw this.

About this time the troops turned and went to the head of Reno Creek and on Reno Creek they separated. The next thing I heard an old man haranguing in the camp, that the soldiers were about to charge the camp from both ends, the upper and the lower. I was in the Cheyenne camp at the lower end of the village.

Then every one who had a horse mounted it. But most of the men were on foot, they had no horses. Reno's party was the first to get down to the Indian camp, and most of the men went up there to meet him. I was with those who went to meet Reno, as he was charging down in the flat where the timber stands. When the troops reached this timber, they went into it and stopped. The Indians were all around them. Then the troops mounted and came out, and when they came out into the flat, the Sioux and Cheyennes charged and the troops ran for the river. The Indians rode right up to them, knocked some of[f] their horses as they were running, and some fell off in the river. It was like chasing buffalo, a grand chase.

Reno's troops crossed the river and got up on the hill. Just as the troops got on the hill, the Indians saw a big pack train of mules coming, which met Reno there. The Indians all stopped at the river; they did not try to cross, but turned back to look over the dead to plunder, and to see who of their own people were killed.

While they were doing this, they heard the shooting and the calling down the river; a man calling out that troops were attacking the lower end of the village. Then they all rushed down below and saw Custer coming down the hill and almost at the river. I was one of the first to meet the troops and the Indians and the soldiers reached the flat about the same time. When Custer saw them coming he was down on the river bottom at the river's bank. The troops formed in line of battle, and there they fought for some little time. Then the troops gave way and were driven up the hill. The troops fought on horseback all the way up the hill; they were on their horses as long as horses lasted, but by this time the Indians had got all around them and they were completely surrounded. Those who were following behind picked up the guns and ammunition belts of the soldiers who had been killed and fought the troops with their own guns. Many of the belts picked up had no cartridges in them. The soldiers were shooting all the time as fast as the Indians. There were so many Sioux and Cheyennes that the whole country seemed to be alive with them, closing in on the troops and shooting. They kept following them up until they got to a high point, and by this time very few white men were left. Here they closed in on them, and in a moment all were killed. I think this ended about two or three o'clock.

After we had killed those on the hill, we discovered that there were some other white men who had got off; they were discovered by people down below, and were below, that is down stream from the monument. They charged these and killed them all.

After they had finished with Custer, they went back to Reno. It was now pretty late in the afternoon. They fought there all night and all the next day until in the middle of the afternoon. While they were fighting, someone came up the river and reported that troops were coming—a good many. They left Reno then and returned to camp, for they made up their mind that they did not want to fight any more. They had fought for two days now and thought that they had fought enough.

Soldier Wolf, Northern Cheyenne, recounted his version of the Little Big Horn to Grinnell in 1898. It is in the Grinnell Collection, Item 497, "Notes on the Custer Fight," Braun Research Library, Southwest Museum, Los Angeles.

I WAS THEN SEVENTEEN YEARS OLD, old enough to notice a great many things and to see the reasons for them. The Cheyennes had been there only for one night; next morning, somewhere about noon, the troops charged down Reno Creek into the upper Sioux village, and drove all the people out and set fire to the lodges. When the people in the lower villages heard the shooting up above, they all rushed toward it, everybody went. The troops retreated, and the Indians all rushed in among them. They were all mixed up. The soldiers seemed to be drunk (probably they were panic stricken); they could not shoot at all. The soldiers retreated to the timber and fought behind cover. If they had remained in the timber, the Indians could not have killed them; but all at once—perhaps they got frightened—they rushed out and started to cross the creek. Then it was that the Indians rushed among them. They [soldiers] crossed the river and went up on a high bluff. When the soldiers got on the ridge, the Indians left them.

When the Indians rushed up to meet Reno, all the women and children gathered down at the lower village, and becoming more and more frightened as they listened to the firing, they decided to cross the river to the east side, and so to get further away from the fight. When these women were crossing the river, and some were going up the hills, they discovered more troops coming—this was Custer's party. The women ran back, and someone rode to where the men were fighting Reno, and told them that more soldiers were coming below. Then all the men rushed down the creek again, to where the women were. By that time, Custer had got down to the mouth of the dry creek, and was on the level flat of the bottom. They began fighting, and for quite a time, fought in the bottom, neither party giving back. There they killed quite a good many horses, and the ground was covered with the horses of Cheyennes, Sioux and of white men, and two soldiers were killed and left here. But soon the Indians overpowered the soldiers and they began to give way, retreating slowly, face to the front. They fell back up the hill until they had come nearly to where the monument now is. Then they turned and rushed over the top of the hill. From this point on, everything was mixed up, for there was a grand charge and nothing clear could be seen for the dust and the people, until all the troops had been killed. Then they ran off all the government horses left alive, eighty or ninety head, down in the creek.

After I had gone down with the horses and the fighting was over, the dust cleared away and I looked toward the hill—where the monument is—and saw many Indians still there. I went back to see what they were doing. As I went back, I found lying along the hill, north of the monument, a number of dead soldiers. When I got on the hill, I found that all the soldiers had been killed.

In the fight, only six Cheyennes were killed dead, some were wounded but not very many. More Sioux were killed and wounded. Reno's men were frightened and acted as if they were drunk—as I think they were. Custer's men fought well and bravely.

The Northern Cheyenne, Tall Bull, furnished the following account of Little Big Horn to George Bird Grinnell in 1898. It is in the Grinnell Collection, Item 497, "Notes on the Custer Fight," Braun Research Library, Southwest Museum, Los Angeles.

ALL THE TROOPS CAME DOWN Reno Creek till they reached a small stream running in from the north; there Custer left and went around to the east. Reno went on, down to Little Sheep Creek [Little Big Horn River], crossed and charged into the upper Sioux village. The people all ran out and the troops set the village on fire.

All the lower village people heard this and rushed up to where the soldiers were. Back of the village that was fired, was a high hill, and the Indians all ran up on it and then charged down on the soldiers, who retreated into the timber. They did not stop there, but ran right through it and out on the other side. I was present there and tried to cross the river. As the troops were crossing the river, the Indians kept killing them right along. When the soldiers had all crossed the stream, news came to the Indians from down the creek, that more soldiers were coming, and all turned back. They did not persue [sic] the soldiers after they had crossed. All rushed back on the west side of the camp, down to a small dry run that comes in from the east, and there, down close to the river, were the soldiers. The Indians all crossed and they fought there. For quite a long time the troops stood their ground right there; then they began to back off, fighting all the time, for quite a distance, working up the hill, until they got pretty close to where the monument now is, and then the soldiers turned and rushed to the top of the hill. There they killed them all.

The horses—a good many—all ran down toward the stream northwest, and the people got about them and ran them off. A few soldiers started to run directly down toward Little Sheep Creek, but the Indians killed them all before they got there. The horse I was riding had seven balls in him and dropped dead under me just before I got to the [area of the present] monument. Six Cheyennes were killed in the fight, but a good many Sioux.

One Bull, Minneconjou Lakota, was the adopted son of the Hunkpapa leader Sitting Bull. Born in 1853, he lived until 1947. His account of the Little Big Horn was given to John P. Everett in the 1920s. It is excerpted here from Sunshine Magazine *11 (September 1930).*

I WAS IN SITTING BULL'S CAMP on [Little] Big Horn River, One Horn Band Hinkowoji [Minneconjou] Tepee. They were called that because they planted their gardens near the river. Itazipco (Without Bow [Sans Arc]) was another band. Ogalala [Oglala] was the Red Cloud band. Another band, Schiyeio means Cheyenne. They were a different tribe, not Lakota. They were friends of Lakota.

Pizi (Gall) had another band. All the different bands camped together. There were many other chiefs with their bands. Four Horn and Two Moon and many others. Whenever the chiefs held a council they went to Sitting Bull's camp because he was a good medicine man.

Lakota and Cheyennes had gone to this camp to look after their buffalo and so young men and women could get acquainted. White men had driven our buffalo away from Lakota land. So we went where buffalo were to take care of them and keep white men away.

I was a strong young man 22 years old. On the day of the fight I was sitting in my tepee combing my hair. I don't know what time it was. About this time maybe. (Two P.M.) Lakota had no watches in those days. I had just been out and picketed my horses and was back in my tepee. I saw a man named Fat Bear come running into camp and he said soldiers were coming on the other side of the river and had killed a boy named Deeds who went out to picket a horse. Then I came out of my tepee and saw soldiers running their horses toward our camp on same side of the river. We could hear lots of shooting. I went to tepee of my uncle, Sitting Bull, and said I was going to go take part in the battle. He said, "Go ahead, they have already fired."

I had a rifle and plenty of shells, but I took that off and gave it to Sitting Bull and he gave me a shield. Then I took the shield and my tomahawk and got on my horse and rode

One Bull, Minneconjou Lakota, 1890s. Photograph by L. W. Stilwell. Courtesy of the Nebraska State Historical Society.

up to where the soldiers were attacking us. They were firing pretty heavy. They were all down near the river in the timber.[6] Lakota were riding around fast and shooting at them. I rode up to some Lakota and said, "Let's all charge at once." I raised my tomahawk and said, "Wakontanka help me so I do not sin but fight my battle." I started to charge. There were five Lakota riding behind me. We charged for some soldiers that were still fighting and they ran to where their horses were in the timber. Then the soldiers all started for the river. I turned my horse and started that way too and there was a man named Mato Washte (Pretty Bear) right behind me and he and his horse were shot down. I followed the soldiers. They were running for the river. I killed two with my tomahawk. Then the soldiers got across the river. I came back to where Pretty Bear was and got him up on my horse. He was wounded and covered with blood. I started my horse toward the river where the soldiers were, trying to get across.

Then I let Pretty Bear get off my horse and I went across the river after the soldiers. I killed one more of them with my tomahawk.

Then I saw four soldiers ahead of me running up the hill. I was just about to charge them when someone rode along beside me and said, "You better not go any farther. You are wounded." That was Sitting Bull. I was not wounded but I was all covered with blood that got on me when I had Pretty Bear on my horse. So I did what Sitting Bull told me. Then Sitting Bull rode back but I went on. Another Lakota went after these four soldiers. He had a rifle and shot one of them off his horse. One of the soldiers kept shooting back but without hitting us. The man that was with me was a Lakota but I did not know who he was. Now the soldiers were getting together up on the hill and we could see the other soldiers coming with the pack mules a long way off.

Then I went back across the river and rode down it a way, then I rode with the man who was shooting at the four soldiers and we crossed the river again just east of Sitting

Two Moon, Northern Cheyenne leader in the Great Sioux War, early 1900s. Photograph by L. A. Huffman. Courtesy of the Montana Historical Society.

Bull's camp. We saw a bunch of horsemen up on a hill to the north and they were Lakotas. We rode up to them and I told them I had killed a lot of soldiers and showed them my tomahawk. Then I said I was going up and help kill Custer's soldiers, but Sitting Bull told me not to go so I didn't go but we rode up where we could see the Lakotas and Cheyennes killing Custer's men. They had been shooting heavy but the Indians charged them straight from the west and then some rode around them shooting and the Indians were knocking them off their horses and killing them with tomahawks and clubs. THEY WERE ALL KILLED. There were a lot of Sioux killed. The others were picking them up on their horses and taking them back to camp.

Then we had a war dance all night and in the morning we heard that the soldiers with the pack mules were up on the hill and the Sioux started up after them. I went with Sitting Bull and volunteered to go help kill these soldiers but Sitting Bull said no. So we watched the fight from a hill. I didn't have my rifle with me then, just my tomahawk. The Sioux surrounded them and they fought that way all day. The soldiers had ditches dug all around the hill. Then along towards sundown the Sioux broke camp and went [south] to the mountains.

The Sioux did not take any prisoners that I know of. I didn't see any. I don't know how many Indians there were, but it was a very big band. Many bands together. The Indians had rifles with little short cartridges. I didn't use mine.

After the fight we all stayed in the Big Horn Mountains about ten days. After that they broke camp and went north following along the Tongue River. Then we went to the Little Missouri, and we found a place where there must have been some soldiers for we found a lot of sacks of yellow corn piled up. Then some of the bands went one way and some went another. One little band went to Slim Buttes and they were all killed by soldiers.

I was with Sitting Bull all the time we were in camp on

the [Little] Big Horn and saw him during the battle. He was telling his men what to do. The first I knew of any soldiers was when they killed the boy who went to picket his horse across the river from Sitting Bull's camp. Before we broke camp that night we saw the walking soldiers coming from down the river but my uncle said, "We won't fight them. We have killed enough. We will go. . . . "

Flying By was a son of Chief Lame Deer of the Minneconjou Lakotas, who was killed late in the Sioux War. Born in 1850, Flying By took an active part in the Battle of the Little Big Horn before later surrendering and residing on the Standing Rock Reservation in South Dakota. His account was given on May 21, 1907, to Walter M. Camp through Interpreter William S. Claymore. It is in Walter Camp Interviews, Box 6, Folder 2, Walter Mason Camp Collection, Archives and Manuscripts, Harold B. Lee Library, Brigham Young University, Provo, Utah.

[WE WERE] IN VILLAGE two or three days before battle. Some Sioux who had lost horses came in and reported Custer coming on trail and Custer showed up not long after Custer's soldiers got there.[7] They called Custer Paonski (Long Hair) and some of Indians thought it might be Custer. Had not been looking for soldiers in that direction.

Soldiers attacked Hunkpapa tepees first. All Indians that had ponies went out to help Hunkpapas fight Reno and some were dismounted. Battle with Reno lasted only short time and my horse shot. Soldiers went through timber and retreated to river. My horse shot and I went back to village for another horse. As soon as Reno retreated more soldiers (Custer) were in sight from village farther down the stream. The soldiers had four or five flags. Custer acted as though would cross and attack village.

We crossed over at all points along river as quick as we could and found Custer already fighting Indians and driving Indians back toward river but when we got over in great numbers Custer was soon surrounded. The soldiers

Flying By, Minneconjou Lakota, 1880s. Photograph by David F. Barry. Courtesy of the State Historical Society of North Dakota.

then got off horses and some let them go and we captured a lot of them. I captured one myself. I took some of the horses to village before battle was over and then came back. Got ammunition from saddles of horses. After came back from taking horses to village I came to gully east of long ridge and many soldiers already killed. . . .

Says Custer's soldiers kept together all the time and were killed moving along toward camp. Killed all way along. Some soldiers still had horses at this time. Did not make any stand except in one place where Custer [was] killed at end of long ridge. Soldiers had plenty of ammunition when killed. Indians closed in and at last part of battle soldiers were running through Indian lines trying to get away. Only four soldiers got into gully toward river.

[Miscellaneous notes:] Hunkpapa and Minneconjou squaws had been taking down tepees during Reno fight. During fight [with Custer] gray horses and others much mixed up. Battle against Custer alone lasted about half the afternoon. After Custer fight we went over and fought soldiers with the pack mules until Indians reported other soldiers coming under officer called the Bear Coat.[8]

[In the Custer fight] soldiers excited and shot wild. We lost only a few men. Did not recognize Custer until some time after the battle and all soldiers killed. Our village the winter before was on Tongue river.

When I got to Custer Indians had been fighting quite awhile. Some of the soldiers let horses go early in fight. Soldiers did not charge after I got there. Four Minneconjous killed. When [we] moved away [we] had considerable ammunition. I had a Winchester rifle with 14 shots. Many of Indians had pump guns. . . . (Heresay—Afterward found two soldiers on Rosebud nearly starved to death. Heard of man who had been eating frogs.)

[After the Little Big Horn battle we] moved toward Big Horn mountains and then back to Rosebud and down that stream.

The account of Little Hawk, Northern Cheyenne, was given to George Bird Grinnell on September 5, 1908. It is in Field

Notebook 348, Grinnell Collection, Braun Research Library, Southwest Museum, Los Angeles.

[FOLLOWING THE ROSEBUD BATTLE the Cheyennes] went back to Reno Creek and stayed one night then moved down to mouth of Reno Creek and stayed there three nights and then moved down on Little Horn and were there one night. The next day Custer made his charge. His presence on Rosebud was reported, but Custer must have traveled as fast as the man who brought the news.

The first charge was made by troops who went down Reno Creek and crossed Little Horn, went down Little Horn about two miles and halted and went down into a low place where water used to stand and where there is timber among the lodges of one of the villages. The Cheyennes charged him [Reno] and he did not stand but charged through them, going back the way he had come. He did not cross where he had come but jumped over a bank. When he had crossed, the Cheyennes did not follow him, for looking back they saw another lot of soldiers coming and they went back to meet them. Little Hawk went back towards Custer. He does not know what became of Reno. Little Hawk went back toward Custer and rode up the little ravine which the Indians went up in approaching Custer. The first thing he saw was Chief Comes in Sight on a bobtail horse riding up and down in front of soldiers who were firing at him. Contrary Belly and Yellow Nose made the first charge. The two rode part way toward the soldiers and turned their horses and came back. Soldiers were all dismounted to fight on foot. As these two came back an officer was killed and fell from his horse and then all the soldiers mounted. Yellow Nose and Contrary Belly now made a second charge and were followed by the rest of the Indians. When they charged, the soldiers ran and went along the straight ridge where they chased them like buffalo and as long as they had their backs toward Indians

Wooden Leg's Drawing of the Seizing of a Soldier's Gun at the Battle of the Little Big Horn. Courtesy of Little Bighorn Battlefield National Monument.

the Indians rode right in among them. At the knoll where the monument stands the soldiers turned and that is the last place he saw them. White Bull's son and [illeg.] Black fell right in among the soldiers as they were going along. White Bull's son lived till next day. Twenty-three [?] dead.

Upon this round knoll, the soldiers having tied their horses in fours, let them go and they scattered, most of them running toward the Little Horn. One company of soldiers went down toward the Little Horn and all but one man dismounted. The one man who did not dismount rode away. He was riding a sorrel horse and Indians began to shoot at him, but they could not hit him nor overtake him. At last, when he was almost out of shot [range], a ball hit him and knocked him off his horse. He is the only man who has not a stone [marker].

In the charge up the ridge where soldiers and Indians were together (when White Bull's son and [illeg.] B were killed) not many soldiers were slain. Most of them got upon the knoll where the monument now stands. From there the most of them were killed by the Indians hidden behind the little ridge, but there was some charging in to these troops by Indians. Yellow Nose captured from a soldier a flag which had a gilt lance head on the staff, the only one of this kind taken. About fifteen flags were captured.

After Custer was finished they went back to Reno to keep him from getting water. They stayed there two days and one [two] night[s]. Then word came that Gen. Miles [Terry] was coming up the Big Horn, but that he had big guns with him. To fight him under such conditions would be merely to waste ammunition for on account of the big guns they could not get close enough to fight him.

The second day in the evening they left Reno and moved camp toward the head of the Little Horn, traveling after night. They do not know when the soldiers came to the place to look at their dead friends. Back when Reno made his charge there were some Ree Indians with him.

When they met in the timber Black Crane's son met a Ree scout (Bloody Knife). These two were riding side by side and pulled triggers at same instant the Cheyenne was killed. . . .

The Northern Cheyenne leader White Bull (Ice) scouted for the soldiers during the later phases of the Sioux War. At the Little Big Horn, however, he led his warriors against Reno and Custer. White Bull provided this statement to George Bird Grinnell in 1895. It is in the Grinnell Collection, Item 497, "Notes on the Custer Fight," Braun Research Library, Southwest Museum, Los Angeles.

RENO CHARGED THE CAMP from below and got in among the lodges of Sitting Bull's camp, some of which he burned, but Reno got frightened and stopped and the Indians caught him and he retreated, as in all the accounts. Then word was brought that Custer was coming, and the Indians all began to go back [downstream] to fight Custer.

Custer rode down to the river bank and formed a line of battle and charged, and then they stopped and fell back up the hill, but he met Indians coming from above and from all sides, and again formed a line. It was here that they were killed.

From the men and from the horses of Reno's command, the Indians had obtained many guns and many cartridges which enabled them to fight Custer successfully. If it had not been for this, they could not have killed them so quickly. It was about eleven o'clock when they attacked Reno, and one o'clock when Custer's force had all been killed. The men of Custer's force had not used many of their cartridges, some had ten cartridges used from their belts and some twenty, but all their saddle pockets were full.

Young Two Moon provided his account of Little Big Horn to George Bird Grinnell in 1908. It is in the Grinnell Collection,

Wooden Leg's Drawing of the Killing of One of Reno's Soldiers at the Battle of the Little Big Horn. Courtesy of Little Bighorn Battlefield National Monument.

Field Notebook 348, Braun Research Library, Southwest Museum, Los Angeles.

HE GUESSES. While fighting Crook on Rosebud the camp moved from head of Reno down a short distance perhaps four miles. After two nights here they moved to mouth of Reno Creek and above mouth of Reno. He thinks they were five or six days in that camp.

While here seven Arapahoes came into camp. They captured them, took their arms and horses and part of their clothing and were going to kill them. Every one believed that these were scouts from some camp of soldiers. Two men took their part — Black Wolf and Last Bull. They said the people should wait and not act hastily. They were taken into Two Moon's lodge, but it was closely surrounded. While there many Sioux came up with cocked guns which they pointed at them saying that they must be killed. Women who had had relatives killed came up crying and asked for the lives of the Arapahoes. Most said this is Two Moon's lodge. Wait till he comes, let him decide. They sent a young man out to look for Old Two Moon. He was found at last in one of the Sioux camps and came. Meantime, while they were searching for Two Moon they took Arapahoes out of lodge. Old Two Moon came to his lodge with five other chiefs and called to the Arapahoes to come in. The chiefs were going to decide what should be done with them.

After they had talked awhile, Old Two Moon called out: "These Arapahoes are all right. They have come here to help us fight the soldiers. Do not harm them but give them back their things." Sioux chiefs called out the same things, and their horses, arms, and clothing were returned. After this some old people called out to take the Arapahoes and let them go to separate lodges and be fed. They divided them and took them away but were directed to bring them back to Two Moon's lodge.

Then they moved camp down below mouth of Reno
Creek and stayed there one night. The next day Custer
came, not early in the morning. John Two Moon was three
miles from where the fight took place and saw it all, but did
not take part in it. His account should therefore give [a]
good general idea of what took place. When he first saw the
soldiers they were just coming down the steep hill east of
battlefield. They were on a lope and Indians were then
behind them but they paid no attention to them. This was
Custer's command. He saw nothing of Reno's battle. It was
out of his sight.

After the soldiers turned upon the little ridge the gray
horse company stopped where [the present] monument is.
The others went on, stopping at intervals until there were
four lines, the last opposite to the camp. After they saw
soldiers there, [Young] Two Moon, who was nearer to the
river on a hillside ran with others and caught their horses
and rushed toward the fight. Several charges had been
made but no fighting had been done. Indians were struggling up the gulch northeast of soldiers like ants rushing
out of a hill.

Yellow Nose made two dashes toward soldiers and
returned and said to his people, "Let us charge." The third
company—the one toward the river—had moved back a
little toward the second. The Indians were trying to drive
the three companies on this ridge running about north and
south over to the gray horse company. Yellow Nose made a
third charge but the other Indians did not follow him.
Meantime, the Indians were getting further to the north
trying to surround soldiers. At the fourth charge, on
Yellow Nose's orders, all Indians mounted and Yellow Nose
made a charge and all Indians followed. They crowded the
company furthest north and they started to run down the
ridge. As they got down part way toward the gray horse
company the latter began to fire and drove Indians off and
the soldiers reached the gray horse company. Some [sol-

Young Two Moon, Northern Cheyenne. Courtesy of the Smithsonian Institution, National Anthropological Archives.

diers] were killed, however, when they reached the gray horse [company]. The latter shot at Indians so fast that they drove Indians back out of sight over hill toward the [location of the later Crow] agency. The same Indians called out very loud, "All dismount,"and they did so. It was done quickly. When Indians dismounted they shot at soldiers who retreated for the top of the hill. Then all Indians mounted and charged. Then the gray horse company turned their horses loose, and some of the horses rushed through the Indians and toward the river. When Indians charged to top of hill they saw the other two companies way down near to the river. Then all the soldiers turned their horses loose. The gray horse company was destroyed on the hill near where they went out of sight. The Indians charged in among them. One of the companies retreated down toward a little gulch where they tried to fight under cover. Here the last of the soldiers were killed. He saw and [?] what the gray horse company did and those who took refuge in the little creek. Those in the creek were all killed before he got there.

If these soldiers had all stood together the Indians could have done nothing with them. The yelling of the Indians seemed to frighten the cavalry horses and they were naying and plundering so that the men could not handle their guns. If the horses, after they had been turned loose, had come to a shallow place in the Little Horn River, they would have crossed it and no one knows when they would have stopped. [Instead,] they struck a deep hole in the river, could not get out on the other side and stayed there swimming around.

The Indian village was a large one and besides there were many young men there. Sioux from as far as the Missouri River were there, all warriors. He guesses that each soldier had to fight about forty men. . . . [Months earlier] they were camped over near Black Hills when they sent runners to call warriors [from] Red Cloud, Spotted Tail, Standing Rock [agencies], etc. Each lodge had from four to six men in it. . . . There were more than 200 lodges

Drawing of Big Beaver, a Northern Cheyenne, Riding among the Dead Custer Soldiers. Courtesy of Little Bighorn Battlefield National Monument.

of Cheyennes and six Sioux camps, each of which was much larger than the Cheyenne camp. There were some Yankton Sioux. This would perhaps make 1700 lodges. Five fighting men to a lodge = 8500 men. . . .

He says that if Custer and Reno had charged through the village from both ends they would have defeated Indians. During night some of the [Reno] soldiers got water somehow without being seen. During the night some [cavalry] horses got loose and ran down to creek where they had crossed to get water. The Indians got them. Next morning one soldier stripped to his underclothing ran down to river and they began to fire at him. He carried a quart cup in one hand and a canteen in the other. When he reached it he threw himself in water, filling his vessels and drinking at the same time. Half the time they could not see him because of the water thrown up by the bullets. Then he ran up the hill again and entered the breastworks unhurt though they had been firing at him all this time.

Next day they [the Indians] stayed there until about 5 o'clock when they heard that soldiers were coming and some of Indians went down to meet them. Then Indians began to leave Reno and called out to move camp. They did so soon and when they had moved off a little way they could see Reno's soldiers going to river. Not far from his breastworks on a little flat Reno put up tents.

Chapter 4

Pursuing Soldiers
in the Big Horns,
July, 1876

*Flying Hawk, Oglala Lakota; Little Sun, Northern
Cheyenne; and Little Hawk, Northern Cheyenne*

*Following the Indians' defeat of Custer, and at the approach of
the soldiers of General Terry and Colonel Gibbon from the
north, the huge Little Big Horn assemblage packed up and
traveled south, towards the Big Horn Mountains in northern
Wyoming Territory. There the various groups began to break off
from the main body seeking game. Some of the tribesmen
hovered near the camp of General Crook near present Sheridan, Wyoming, and in early July they encountered a scouting
party from Crook's command composed of soldiers and civilian
guides. These troops, under Lieutenant Frederick W. Sibley,
received a scare when the Indians surrounded them on the edge
of the mountains and exchanged gunfire with them. The encounter represented the first contact between Sioux and Cheyenne
warriors and the troops since the Indians had destroyed Custer.*

*Remarkably, two, and possibly three, of the warriors who
participated in the attack on Sibley's party left reminiscent
accounts. The following is that of Moses Flying Hawk (1852–
1931), an Oglala Sioux, who provided his recollections of the
event to Eli S. Ricker on March 8, 1907. The transcript is in the
Ricker Collection, Tablet 13, Microfilm Roll 3, Nebraska State
Historical Society, Lincoln.*

MOSES FLYING HAWK, a Sioux Indian, speaking of the
Sibley Scout, said:

That he was one of the attacking party where the
scouts abandoned their horses, which party was composed

Flying Hawk, Oglala Lakota, ca. 1902. Photograph by W. J. Nichols. Courtesy of the Nebraska State Historical Society.

of about nineteen (19) Indians, which was augmented by reinforcements constantly arriving. A watch was kept up all night by the Indians at the point where the attack was made. He says the scouts got away by deserting their horses and ascending the mountain. Among these Indian reinforcements were some Cheyennes, one of whom was killed, as was stated by Big Bat [Pourier, a white guide with the army command]. Flying Hawk rubbed his hands together as the Indians do to indicate complete destruction, saying that was what would have been the fate of the scouts if they had not sneaked away, as they did, at a timely hour.

An account from the Northern Cheyenne perspective is that of Little Sun, who gave his recollections to George Bird Grinnell on August 7, 1916. The transcript reposes in the George Bird Grinnell Collection, Field Notebook 354, Braun Research Library, Southwest Museum, Los Angeles.

LITTLE SUN CAME to camp. He was with people attacking Sibley outfit when High Bear was killed. He says: After the Crook [Custer] fight the day of Sibley encounter about one-half men in camp had gone out to chase buffalo. A young man wandering about had come across trail of Sibley party and returned to camp and reported it. Most of men in camp went out to see what it was. They found the soldiers, but kept out of sight waiting for troops to go into a good place to attack. Troops traveled on and presently stopped and dismounted. Cheyennes went around the mountain a little farther beyond and there got behind a knoll and waited for troops to come into this park. Troops came into park but just as they entered it the returning buffalo hunters who knew nothing of troops presence came in sight. The Cheyennes who were waiting knew that troops would discover buffalo hunters and some [felt] obliged to charge without waiting for troops to get into the position where Cheyennes wanted them. Cheyennes charged and troops went into timber and Cheyennes retreated. They shot at each other a little, neither side seeing the other. Then some one of Cheyennes proposed a charge. They charged up to timber and split, one half going to left and the other to the right. Those at right went

Spotted Blackbird

at Crow Agency, 1926.
Cheyenne Veterans of the Custer Battle, 1876.

Braided Locks

Bad Horse

Hollow Wood

Wolf Name

Photo June 26, 1926
by Thomas B. Marquis

Porcupine

In council, at 50th anniversary celebration of the Custer battle.
Question: "Shall we join in the ceremony where all old-time enemies shake hands?"
Decision: "No. Let us wait until we are paid for our Black Hills lands."

Cheyenne Warrior Veterans of the Battle of the Little Big Horn at the Fiftieth Anniversary Observance, 1926. Left to right: Porcupine, Spotted Blackbird, Braided Locks, Bad Horse, Hollow Wood, and Wolf Names. Photograph by Thomas B. Marquis.

on some distance [and] entered timber and there two men were sent forward on foot to find if they could see the soldiers. When they returned they reported that they could see the horses standing tied, but no men. Cheyennes rode through timber to another park and then under cover of some rocks approached near horses and shot into timber but there was no reply. Later they repeated this and a few shots were fired from timber and High Bear who had shown himself was shot. He called out "I am killed" and died.

The troops were thus in real danger, for Indians were on both sides of them. If they had gone in any direction than the one they took, Cheyennes would have caught and probably have killed them all. Cheyennes took away body of High Bear, tied it on a horse and took it to the camp. It must have been the next day that Sioux came up there and found the horses tied up there.

Another Cheyenne remembrance was provided by Little Hawk, who may or may not have been a participant in the fight but who definitely was with his people during the movements after Little Big Horn. Little Hawk responded to George Bird Grinnell in 1908. His statement is in the Grinnell Collection, Notebook 348, Braun Research Library, Southwest Museum, Los Angeles.

SOME YOUNG MEN were sent out to hunt game. As they were killing buffalo this young man saw soldiers and reported it. The camp then moved in part and traveled, but not together but in sections. When day came they saw the soldiers at the foot of Big Horn Mountains. Soldiers saw them and went up into Big Horn Mountains and Indians followed them. They overtook them on the rocks and charged them. Soldiers went into thick timber and dismounted and they could do nothing with them. One Indian was killed: High Bear. They killed no soldiers. There were lots of soldiers on Tongue River [Crook's camp

Lakota Survivors of the Little Big Horn, 1948. Left to right: Iron Hail, High Eagle, Iron Hawk, Little Warrior, Comes Again, Pemmican, and Standing Bull. Courtesy of Little Bighorn Battlefield National Monument.

on Goose Creek] but Indians never disturbed them. Next day some Indians came along and went into the timber and found all the horses tied there and took them all. The Cheyennes after the fight did not go into the timber.

Chapter 5
The Skirmish at Warbonnet Creek, July 17, 1876

Beaver Heart, Northern Cheyenne, and Josie Tangleyellowhair, Northern Cheyenne

While events unfolded on the plains of southeastern Montana, Indians at the agencies of the Great Sioux Reservation, who swiftly learned of these activities, grew uneasy following the victories of their kinsmen over Crook and Custer. In reaction, Sioux warriors and their families departed the Missouri River agencies to support their relatives in the Yellowstone country. Other Indians left the Red Cloud and Spotted Tail agencies in Nebraska.

It was a movement of tribesmen from the Red Cloud Agency that precipitated the first clash between the Indians and a major army command since the Little Big Horn. In mid-July a group of two hundred Cheyennes under Little Wolf left Red Cloud Agency intending to strike north across Wyoming and join the scattering tribes. On the morning of July 17, the advance members of this body were surprised and repelled by troops of the Fifth Cavalry under Colonel Wesley Merritt. The encounter produced a legendary component of the war when a young Cheyenne named Yellow Hair received mortal wounds by the hand of Scout William F. (Buffalo Bill) Cody in an incident touted by the eastern media as "the First Scalp for Custer." The Cheyennes withdrew before Merritt's soldiers all the way back to Red Cloud Agency.

The following Cheyenne recollections recount the Warbonnet Creek skirmish. The first is by Beaver Heart, a member of the war party who was twenty-four years old in 1876. The second, by Josie Tangleyellowhair, presents the unique perspective of the event by the sister of the warrior killed by Cody. Both accounts, interpreted by Willis Rowland on May 27, 1929, at Lame Deer, Montana, repose in the James H. Cook Collection, Scotts Bluff National Monument, Scottsbluff, Nebraska.

A BAND OF CHEYENNES (Little Wolf's band) were at the old Red Cloud Agency at Ft. Robinson Nebraska. Shortly after the Custer battle on the Little Big Horn we heard about this fight and started to go from Ft. Robinson to the scene of this fight.

We traveled all day and that night camped on War Bonnet Creek. After we made camp Chief Little Wolf appointed three of us to go out and scout ahead in the direction we were traveling to see if there were any soldiers near. The three appointed were myself (Beaver Heart), Buffalo Road, and Yellow Hair. We scouted around all that night and early in the morning we were on a high bluff or hill and looked down and saw two [seven] troops of United States cavalry. These soldiers were just saddling up and getting ready to leave. The bluff we were on overlooked War Bonnet Creek and the soldiers were camped on this creek.

We immediately returned to the camp and reported that soldiers were near and we told them where they were at. I and seven other warriors on horseback started over to where the soldiers were. We saw a man on horseback riding back and forth upon the same ridge we were on when first sighting the soldiers. We proceeded toward this hill and the man we saw then disappeared and went down the other side. We started to climb the hill and were almost on the top. When we were almost at the top of this hill the soldiers suddenly appeared on the top of the hill and began firing at us, and we ran back toward the main body of Indians. The soldiers followed us and kept shooting at us as we retreated. Two of the warriors left us and started up the Creek. Pretty soon my horse was hit and fell dead and I was afoot. The other five warriors left me and rode back to the main body of Indians. I was in rough country and worked my way on foot toward the head of the soldiers who were stretched over quite a bit of country. I thought that I could fight better and stand less chance of getting hit if I was at the head of the soldiers.

I was there firing at the soldiers with a six shooter as I had no rifle, and pretty soon Yellow Hair rode up to where I was and asked me how I was, and told me that we had to do some fighting to keep the soldiers away from the women and children. He then rode down the line of the soldiers away from us. The soldiers were firing at him all the time, but he reached the end of the line of soldiers before his horse was killed. His horse was killed then and Yellow Hair jerked the bridle off his dead horse and took his war bonnet off and tucked it under his belt. He then started to walk off. The soldiers were firing at him. The bullets were flying all around him, and he didn't go far before he was hit and fell dead. After he was killed the soldiers quit firing, and then one soldier dismounted and went over to where he laid and reached down and got his war bonnet and lifted it up in the air and was shaking it. Then another man came up to where Yellow Hair laid and sit down near his head. We were too far away to see what he was doing. The first man to reach his body was a Sergeant we could tell by the yellow stripes on his arms. The second man did not have a uniform on. Yellow Hair was scalped but we did not know who done it. Pretty soon we saw a fire blazing where Yellow Hair's body was and the soldiers drew away.

After Yellow Hair was killed I got up and went over to where the other Indians were. They thought I had been killed and when I returned they were glad to see me and they all shook my hand. The soldiers were in front of us and we couldn't go ahead so we all started back toward the agency (Ft. Robinson). The soldiers did not fire upon us, but they kept behind us as we were going back. While they were driving us back, some of the warriors sneaked out and circled around the soldiers. I was one of them that did this. Those that sneaked out bunched up and kept traveling and we ran across another bunch of Cheyennes in the mountains near where the town of Glendive [Montana] is now located. The next day after the fight some of Yellow Hair's relatives went and saw his body. I wasn't there and don't know what they done with his body.

I want to say in conclusion that I do not know Buffalo Bill (Pa-he-haska). I have heard the story as related by him regarding this fight and the fact that Yellow Hair challenged him. This is not true. Buffalo Bill, who ever he was, could not talk Cheyenne and Yellow Hair could not talk English or Sioux, and I do not know how these two people could talk to each other. Furthermore, Yellow Hair was not killed by any one man as far as I could see as the whole two [seven] troops of soldiers were firing at him. If Buffalo Bill was with these soldiers he stayed with them until Yellow Hair was killed, and he did not come out and engage Yellow Hair single handed.

I, JOSIE TANGLEYELLOWHAIR, eighty-seven years old, and a member of the Northern Cheyenne tribe of Indians, a full sister of Yellow Hair (Yellow Hand), make the following statement in regard to the killing of my brother, Yellow Hair, by soldiers on War Bonnet Creek near old Ft. Robinson in Nebraska.

A band of Cheyennes were camped at Ft. Robinson and I was with this band. There was also another band besides us at this Ft. Robinson, and they were called Rough Faces. This band of Rough Faces were outlawed or ostracized, and were not allowed to camp with the main band at Ft. Robison [sic] because they were the ones who were charged with having stolen a horn from the sacred buffalo head. Beaver Heart was a member of this Rough Face band.

When we left Ft. Robinson and encountered soldiers at War Bonnet Creek, I remember that Plenty Camps, an uncle of Beaver Heart, was the only member of the Rough Face band to accompany us. Beaver Heart states that he made his home with his Uncle, Plenty Camps, and if such is the case he must have been camped with us at the place on War Bonnet Creek where the skirmish took place, as I remember seeing Plenty Camps there.

I do not remember seeing Beaver Heart at this camp on War Bonnet Creek. I remember that Yellow Hair, my brother, and Buffalo Road, my uncle, were appointed to go out scouting for soldiers, and I do not know who else was appointed to go with them. Yellow Hair and Buffalo Roads saddled their horses and left from our tent, and I did not see them leave camp and do not know who went with them. The camp was scattered around and it might be possible that they picked up Beaver Heart before leaving on this scouting trip.

The actual skirmish occurred some distance from the camp, and as the soldiers fired many shots no one knew who killed my brother. An Indian by the name of White Horse was the one that informed me that Yellow Hair had been killed by the soldiers.

According to the general opinion and talk of the Indians, Yellow Hair was killed by one of the bullets fired by the soldiers and was not killed in single combat with Buffalo Bill. The actual skirmish occurred away from the main camp and no one at the camp saw the fight, but we could hear the shots fired. In the excitement and confusion at camp it was hard to find out the details of the fight. About a month after this skirmish some of my relatives went and found Yellow Hair's body, and at that time there wasn't anything left but his bones, but we could see by marks on his skull that he had been scalped.

Chapter 6
The Battle of Slim Buttes, September 9, 1876

Red Horse, Minneconjou Lakota; Charger, Two Kettle Lakota; Many Shields, Sans Arc Lakota; and Tall Bull, Northern Cheyenne

The large body of Indians that had defeated Custer continued to fragment into smaller groups in the weeks after their victory. While the main group of Northern Cheyennes congregated in Wyoming Territory along the headwaters of the Little Big Horn, Big Horn, and Tongue rivers, the various Lakota tribes, along with some Cheyennes, drifted northeast. Some headed immediately for the buffalo grounds north of the Yellowstone. Others hunted the Tongue–Powder River country. Still others drifted east, intent either on going into the agencies or on trading in the region of the Black Hills. These latter tribesmen planned to return to the Yellowstone to seek game before the onset of winter. The eastern migrants included the large followings of Sitting Bull and Crazy Horse.

By early September the Lakotas had located in the area of Grand River in present-day northwest South Dakota. One small village under Iron Plume (American Horse) encamped beneath the sheltering heights of Slim Buttes, a mud and limestone escarpment that afforded security and promised good hunting. There, on September 9, a detachment from Crook's army surprised them at dawn. Most of the Indians—warriors as well as noncombatants—fled in the misty twilight, although some took refuge in a ravine near the village and held out against the troops for several hours. After Crook's main command arrived on the scene, Indians from the distant camp appeared and opened a long-range engagement that was eventually quelled by darkness. Next day the soldiers, buoyed by the first major army success in the Sioux War and sustained by foodstuffs from the Indian camp, marched south toward the Black Hills.

The following accounts describe the events at Slim Buttes from several perspectives. They include both immediate and reminiscent testimony. That of Red Horse, a prominent Minneconjou leader who was forty-one years old in 1876, is contained in Colonel W. H. Wood to Assistant Adjutant General, Department of Dakota, February 27, 1877, Sioux War Papers, National Archives, Record Group 94 (Records of the Adjutant General's Office), Microfilm M666, Roll 280.

AFTER THE GREASY GRASS CREEK fight we all moved east until we came near Slim Buttes. The Indians decided after this [Little Big Horn] fight that there was nothing to be gained by fighting two large bodies of troops, but that there was something gained by having them follow us until their horses gave out, for then they could do us no harm. When the two commands [of Terry and Crook] divided we made a stand for one of them, but for some reason they passed us and did not attack us. I left the main camp then with forty-eight lodges and camped at Slim Buttes. There I was attacked by the troops. It was early in the morning, still dark and misting. We were all asleep. The first we knew we were fired upon, we caught up what arms we could find in the dark, the women taking the children and hiding among the rocks. We gathered up a few horses and put our families on them and went to the main camp, about a day's journey distant, where we told what had happened. A large body of young men went out in pursuit. These troops were from the Platte. We were coming in here to stay—to give ourselves up, the same as we have done now—when we were attacked. Seven of my people were killed and four wounded at that time. Some of my horses were shot. The troops captured all our lodges, all our buffalo robes, and we had a great many. They took all we had. The main body [of Indians] then left Slim Buttes and traveled to the Yellowstone where they camped a little below the mouth of Tongue river.

Charger, later known as Samuel Charger, a Two Kettle Lakota,
offered a reminiscence of Slim Buttes, as published in Sunshine
Magazine 10 (Dec. 1928). He was seventeen years old in 1876.

SOME OF THE NON-HOSTILE BAND, who were receiving
rations at the Agency, went north to the Slim Butte country in the spring of 1876. There was forty-four families in
this band. As they were returning to the reservation that
fall, probably in September, and when they were camped
at the east of the Slim Buttes and as General Custer was
killed, it was thought that some one from this camp should
go to the Agency and investigate. It seemed to them that
everything was up-side down. They also had heard of the
ponies that were taken away by military forces and it was
agreed that the following should go and find out as to
whether it would be safe to go back on the reservation.
Don't Touch It, Standing Bull, Black Horse, Hunts Enemy
and they were encamped waiting for the return of the
above-named Indians when General Crook was returning
from the Sioux campaign in the north that summer. Scouts
informed General Crook about the Sioux camp at Slim
Butte and at day break on the next day the soldiers made a
raid on the camp. Troops of cavalry ran into the camp while
the Indians were yet sleeping, and commenced to fire into
them. The Indians fled naked, some of their ponies stampeded and all of the ponies were taken by the soldiers,
except a few which ran in the direction of the fleeing
Indians were not taken. As some of these ponies were
caught by the Indians some rode double on their ponies
and made their escape. All their tents, food, and other
articles such as beadwork were destroyed by fire, leaving
some of the fleeing Indians almost helpless, and in a
destitute condition.

When they were assembled that day they found out
that the following Indians were killed: Rushe's, First Generation, Split, and a boy named Soldier, and four women

and one infant child. Charging Bear and his wife and also
the wife of Don't Touch It were carried away captives. A
boy was wounded on his left foot and was left in the camp.
The soldiers took him to their camp and kept him there
that day. He was released but he could not walk, but later
was found. The warrior Burnt Thigh took word to the main
hostile camp and the warriors made a charge on Crook that
day.

The main hostile camp which killed Custer, was in
camp to the north of Slim Butte when this massacre [*sic*]
took place. The Minnekauwoji [Minneconjou], Oglala and
Sans Arc bands were in the fight but the fight ended
without any serious killing on either side. The captives
were taken to Rosebud [Spotted Tail] Agency.

[Don't] Touch It after he returned went in quest of his
wife and the other captives. When he got to Rosebud
reservation Chief Spotted Tail, being a relative, assisted
him in getting the captives released, and he brought them
back, after the massacre of Slim Butte. Some of them came
back but a few who were yet suspicious stayed with the
hostile bands.

*Many Shields, a Sans Arc Sioux, provided an immediate account
of Slim Buttes, although it should be noted that he was not
present during the battle. Many Shields discussed his family's
fate as a result of the army attack, and his statement is supple-
mented by information provided by Indian scouts for the army.
The account is contained in Lieutenant Colonel George P. Buell
to the Assistant Adjutant General, Department of Dakota,
September 19, 1876, National Archives, Record Group 393
(Records of United States Army Continental Commands, 1821–
1920). Item 7215.*

[MANY SHIELDS] IS THE HUSBAND of Swelled Woman and
his daughter is the Yellow Haired Woman. His wife,
daughter and one son were part of a party of Indians
captured near Slim Buttes on or about the 9th of Septem-

ber. (It is supposed by a part of General Crook's command.) He had come in to find out on what terms they could come in. When he got back he found the camp had been attacked, and all killed except those captured, and supposed his wife, daughter, and son to be among the captured.[9]

They are Sans Arcs and belong to Crow Feather's band. Many Shields was in, then went out to see if any of the hostiles would come in. Came in again to see what would be done with them, and when he went back the last time, found that this camp had been attacked. I would respectfully request that if his people are among those captured, they be returned to him, as I regard him one of the Indians who try to do right. Many Shields has been in and out, trying to get his family in. He has not been engaged in any of the fights. To confirm this report of Many Shields, my scouts who left here on the 9th for the purpose of communicating, if possible, with General Terry, returned last night. At White Butte they struck a large cavalry trail leading south. Following this trail they came to Slim Buttes, where they discovered that the cavalry had fought and burned a camp of forty lodges; they saw the remnant of guns, robes, and kettles burned. Before arriving at Slim Buttes the scouts saw the [major] hostile camp of the Indians, spoken of in my dispatch of this date. An Indian named The Man Who Hurts Himself, and who accompanied the scouts, first discovered it from a high hill, and called their attention to it, which they say contained three or four thousand lodges. They laid by until dark, when they passed the camp. The trail of the cavalry passed within seven miles of this large camp, but they say from all appearances it must have been raining at the time.

At Slim Butte where this fight occurred, they discovered a large Indian pony trail of about two thousand ponies following after the cavalry trail; it was not more than an hour or two old. They followed on and found two soldiers who had been buried and dug up, horribly mutilated; showing there must have been another fight. Still following this trail they found a squaw who had escaped from the troops. She told them that at Slim Butte the troops had burned up about forty lodges and taken all their horses, killed ten Indians and captured nine. Some Indians made their escape, got to the main hostile camp, and reported this affair. About two thousand warriors started in pursuit. So reported.

When they overtook the cavalry a running fight took place, in which she made her escape. The cavalry trail appeared to be very large; found many dead horses on the trail with their hams cut out, as though the troops or Indians had been subsisting on them. This squaw reports that the Indians recaptured from the troops about three hundred head of horses.[10] The Indian, The Man Who Hurts Himself, says from appearances there must have been three fights after the Indians from the hostile camp started in pursuit of the cavalry.

The Indians say that these hostiles turned back at the foot of the Black Hills and the command made their escape. This trail of the troops and Indians, the scouts report, was going in the direction of the Black Hills. I think there is no doubt that a fight has occurred between some of our troops and a party of hostiles. How it ended can only be conjectured (as all the information is from the Indians) until you get the reports from the proper officers.

The Northern Cheyenne, Tall Bull, provided a brief statement of his role in the relief party from the Grand River village that engaged the soldiers on the afternoon of September 9. Given to Walter M. Camp on July 22, 1910, through interpreter Thaddeus Redwater, the statement is in the Walter Camp Interview Notes, Box 4, Walter Mason Camp Collection, Archives and Manuscripts, Harold B. Lee Library, Brigham Young University, Provo, Utah.

Tall Bull, Northern Cheyenne, 1920s. Courtesy of Jerome A. Greene.

THE SLIM BUTTE FIGHT was with a small party of Sioux who were detached from the main Indian camp and they were out deer hunting. At that time there were ten or a dozen small detached parties of Indians out hunting. The soldiers struck this camp and massacred the people. Some ran to us and we attacked the soldiers and fought most of the day. Tall Bull says that some of the men who ran from the end of the ridge to the gully were firing their guns at random.

Chapter 7
The Spring Creek Encounters, October 11, 15–16, 1876
Lazy White Bull, Minneconjou Lakota

Within weeks of the Slim Buttes affair, most of the tribesmen had migrated west from the vicinity of Grand River in Dakota Territory. Those with Crazy Horse and other chiefs, principally Oglalas, gravitated towards their Powder River hunting grounds below the Yellowstone. Those with Sitting Bull, largely Hunkpapas, Minneconjous, and Sans Arcs, headed northwest, eventually fording the low waters of the Yellowstone to hunt the buffalo herds that roamed north of that stream each autumn. It was this latter group that next encountered the soldiers.

After Crook, Terry, and Gibbon withdrew from the campaign in the late summer and fall of 1876, only Colonel Nelson A. Miles and his command remained in the war zone, under orders to build a cantonment along the Yellowstone at the mouth of Tongue River and to occupy it through the winter. Another cantonment stood on the north side of the Yellowstone opposite the mouth of Glendive Creek some 140 miles east of the Tongue. With soldiers of the Fifth and Twenty-second Infantry regiments, Miles prepared to vigorously prosecute the Lakotas and the Cheyennes.

Sitting Bull's warriors viewed the army presence as a constraint to their continued occupation of the country; moreover, they became particularly incensed when military supply trains running between Glendive Creek and Tongue River frightened the game and disrupted their hunting. During mid-October Sioux anxiety erupted with attacks on the Glendive-to-Tongue wagon train near Spring Creek. Indian accounts of the episode are rare. That offered below was given by Lazy White Bull (Joseph White Bull), a Minneconjou nephew of Sitting Bull, to Stanley Vestal (Walter Stanley Campbell), during the 1920s. It is excerpted from Vestal, Warpath: The True Story of the Fighting Sioux Told in a Biography of Chief Joseph White Bull *(Boston: Houghton Mifflin Company, 1934).*

ON THE NIGHT OF OCTOBER 10, the Sioux stampeded and captured forty-seven mules from the camp of Captain C. W. Miner and four companies of infantry, and next morning, when the crippled train tried to advance, the Indians quickly forced it to turn back. As soon as that happened, the Sioux let the wagons go: all they asked was to be let alone. But the civilian teamsters were so terrified that they refused to go with the train a second time; they had to be replaced by enlisted men. Then the train started out again.

Four days later [October 15], White Bull learned that soldiers were coming again. He stripped to the gee-string and put on his fine war-clothes. He thrust each sinewy leg into a dark blue woolen leggin, decorated with handsome stripes of blue-and-white beadwork, and fastened the straps to his belt on either side. Under his belt, before and behind, he tucked a bright strip of scarlet flannel hanging to his ankles. Then he pulled over his head a white buckskin shirt and around it buckled his cartridge-belt, heavy with cartridges of red metal. Over his right shoulder he slung his war-charm, so that the eagle feather and buffalo tail attached to it swung under his left arm. In his black hair he fastened two upright eagle feathers, lustrous white with black tips, and, carrying his Winchester, stepped outside the tipi. There stood his war-horse, a spirited pinto, red and white, reared from a foal by his mother. He tied up its tail in flannel red as blood, and attached two eagle feathers there. Then he bridled the horse with a bridle decorated at the brow-band with eagle feathers and at the bit with a flaunting tassel of woman's hair, evidence that this horse had been used to run down an enemy. Folding his blanket, he laid it on the animal's bare back. Then he mounted his eager war-horse and rode out with eight companions.

Somewhat later, they heard shooting over the hill and, quirting their ponies, rode to the sound of the guns.

From the hilltop they saw wagons, with many soldiers on foot all around them. The Sioux were riding around, trying to get at the wagons, but the soldiers would not let them. All the Sioux were on horseback.

The wagons never stopped; they kept right on going. All the time the footsoldiers were charging back at the Indians, and then running to catch up with the wagons, and the Sioux were all around, circling and shooting and yelling. White Bull saw his friends firing into these soldiers. He did not know why, but he did not pause to ask questions. He charged right into the middle of the fight. Afterward someone told him: "We saw these wagons and rode down to ask them for something to eat, we were hungry. But the soldiers started shooting, and that's the way the fight began."

For a while White Bull was in the thick of it. He rode up within seventy-five yards of the wagons, looking for a chance to charge in and count *coup*. The soldiers were firing all the time, and there were a lot of them, nearly two hundred. Then the first thing White Bull knew, he was shot. He was hit in the left upper arm. The bullet went clear through and broke the bone. He wears the scar still. The shock of the wound knocked White Bull out. But he stuck on his horse, and right away two of his friends came and led him back to camp. The only other Indian wounded in this skirmish was Broken Leg; he was shot in the sole of the foot. Bad Hair's son was killed. The fight did not last long.

But it was a hot fight while it lasted. There was much shooting. The Indians made a most determined attack. They set the short grass of the prairie afire. The wagons had to advance through the flames. They moved in four lines close together, surrounded by the infantry escort. Every once in a while the Indians would see a soldier fall, then his comrades would carry him and put him into one of the wagons. Four soldiers were wounded that day. . . . .

Sitting Bull did not approve of all this fighting. He wished to hunt in peace. Accordingly next day [October 16, after further skirmishing had occurred] he told Johnny Brughiere [Bruguier, a mixed-blood who was living with the Indians and who later scouted for Miles] he wished to write a letter to the white soldier chief. Brughiere took a piece of white cloth and said he was ready to act as Sitting Bull's clerk. Sitting Bull dictated as follows:

Friend:
I am coming up here to hunt. Ever since I was grown I have been unwilling to fight with soldiers or white men. But wherever I camp, you come and begin shooting at me. Now again you are shooting at me, but still I have come only for hunting. Therefore, when you see my letter, move away. I am coming there to hunt.
                                                I am Sitting Bull.

The note was left in sight of the soldiers in a cleft stick:

YELLOWSTONE
I want to know what you are doing on this road. You scare all the buffalo away. I want to hunt in this place. I want you to turn back from here. If you don't, I will fight you again. I want you to leave what you have got here and turn back from here. I am your friend.
                                                SITTING BULL
I mean all the rations you have got and some powder. Wish you would write as soon as you can.

When Colonel E. S. Otis [commanding the train escort] received this note, a conference was held. Three chiefs talked for Sitting Bull. Otis made them a present of one hundred and fifty pounds of hard bread and two sides of bacon. He said he had no authority to treat with them, but suggested that the Indians could go to the mouth of Tongue River to make peace. The Sioux did not molest the train further.

Chapter 8

The Cedar Creek Councils and the Battle of Cedar Creek, October 20–21, 1876

Long Feather, Hunkpapa Lakota, and Bear's Face, Blackfeet Lakota; Spotted Elk, Minneconjou Lakota; and Lazy White Bull, Minneconjou Lakota

Sitting Bull's people turned north after the encounters with the troops from the Glendive Cantonment. The soldiers moved on to Tongue River. But Colonel Nelson A. Miles, who had departed the Tongue River Cantonment with his Fifth Infantrymen to relieve the tardy wagon train, determined to follow the tribesmen north. Along the upper reaches of Cedar Creek, Sitting Bull agreed to meet the colonel in conference—the first meeting of a federal representative with a leader of the Indian coalition since the beginning of the Sioux War. The councils of October 20 and 21 were important: they indicated to Miles the condition and temperament of Sitting Bull's people while signifying to the Sioux the earnestness of the troops in bringing the so-called hostiles to bay.

Following the protracted councils, which did not produce Sitting Bull's capitulation, the Hunkpapa leader arrayed his warriors on the hills and awaited Miles's assault, which was not long in coming. The Cedar Creek battle melted into a pursuit of the tribesmen toward the Yellowstone River, where many of them agreed to surrender. Sitting Bull, with his immediate followers, headed north again, towards the Fort Peck Indian Agency on the Missouri River.

The following three accounts offer Sioux perspectives on the events surrounding the Cedar Creek councils, some particulars of the resultant battle, and its aftermath. The first consists of a statement by Long Feather and Bear's Face, Hunkpapa and Blackfeet Lakota scouts, respectively, who had been sent from Standing Rock Agency to induce Sitting Bull to surrender. These

97

men had first appeared during Otis's fight with the Indians.
During the protocol preceding the councils, they served as
intermediaries between Sitting Bull and Miles. Their undated
account (ca. November 1876), with the interpreter unidentified,
was submitted by Lieutenant Colonel William P. Carlin, Seven-
teenth Infantry, commanding at Standing Rock Agency, Dako-
ta. It is in the National Archives, Record Group 393 (Records of
United States Army Continental Commands, 1821–1920), De-
partment of Dakota, Item 3394.

WE CAMPED TEN NIGHTS; on the eleventh night saw
men—ten nights without seeing anyone. We got to the old
camp where the hostiles were, followed their trail. Sitting
Bull said, of all the different posts on the river, here you
excel in sending anyone out. We have gone out and succeeded in doing what you wanted done. Heard that men
had been fighting out there. The troops had been moving
up the Yellowstone and troops had been fighting. Saw
Indians. Went to the village of Sitting Bull and he called
me cousin and wanted to know what I came out to him for.
Sitting Bull and his warriors were in council with me one
day and night. They were well pleased and said they did
not want to fight. I took my papers and went to the
soldiers. The commanding officer [Otis] treated me well.
He was moving up [the Yellowstone to] Tongue River with
his troops. He gave me some hard bread, sugar and coffee.
He asked me if the Indian he saw was Sitting Bull. I told
him yes and he said to "bring him to me." I took Sitting
Bull by the hand and took him to the soldiers and made
him shake him by the hands.[11]

Colonel Otis told him that he (Bear's Face) had "done
a great thing;"—that they made peace between this body
of soldiers and all Sitting Bull's band. Bear's Face asked
Colonel Otis to report these proceedings. That Sitting Bull
and his people are coming to this Standing Rock Agency to
make peace, but now, when they see these Indians running away, he don't know what the effect . . . [will be?]

Long Feather, Hunkpapa Lakota, 1880s. Photograph by David F. Barry. Courtesy of the State Historical Society of North Dakota.

The next day after the interview the camp moved eastwardly towards Tongue River. While hunting buffalo they heard that white men were coming towards their camp. Sitting Bull came to them and wanted them to go again with him to the whites. The whites (Colonel Miles) came in a body and the Indians went in a body, and they met in council. These troops were on the war-path—we ran great risk in going to them, but we went directly to them. (We) Bear's Face, Uncpapa, and Long Feather, Blackfeet, went to meet them first. The commanding officer told us to bring Sitting Bull to meet him, so we went back to camp and told Sitting Bull that we wanted him to go with us to meet the troops again. Sitting Bull took his most prominent men and went to the troops and then followed another hand shaking. Sitting Bull took a fine robe and spread it out and asked the chief white men to sit on it. They smoked a pipe of peace. Sitting Bull took a pipe and went through the Indian ceremony of making peace. Sitting Bull declared his intention to quit fighting, lay down his arms and make peace with the government. Sitting Bull told the officers, pointing to the buffalo robe, that that was what he was raised with; the whites would never agree to what he said and that was why he had never consented to go to white men's houses, but now this robe should be the emblem, or bond, of his willingness to make a treaty of peace.

Sitting Bull said, "I now agree to make a treaty and with the intention of keeping it, but I am suspicious of you and fear that you will break it" and that he always maintained that the whites had always been the aggressors. "Since ever I was a child I have treated traders well. I considered them my friends and I have had dealings with them." Here the white chief (supposed to be Colonel Miles) told him that he would use his influence to have an Agency for him established on Tongue River, with a Trader for his people.

Sitting Bull told him that if the whites had contented themselves with taking possession of the Black Hills he would have let them alone, but they not only stole that country but chased him and his people through the country. Sitting Bull said if the white[s] and Indians would meet in council and draw up agreements between them, all would be well; that this was the seventh talk he had had with whites, but he had never yet concluded a satisfactory agreement for his people. Sitting Bull said now he wanted to go to an agency, but he didn't want to go to an agency and lay down his arms while the troops remained in the country. The officer asked Sitting Bull if he could take with him all the Indians in this country. He said he could. Sitting Bull asked the officer if he could remove the troops; the officer said he could have it done.

Sitting Bull stated that he wanted to retain the privilege of trading with traders. Sitting Bull said that some one had come to the command of Standing Rock Agency who could see; that he had chosen two men who were equal to the task imposed upon them of bearing messages to a great nation. Sitting Bull said "I point the stem of this pipe to the Great Spirit. He thinks nothing bad. I believe that he is near us and looking down upon us. We are agreeing to keep the peace and smoke this pipe together. The Great Spirit is a witness to this peace, but I am afraid you will break it. The people, when they make an agreement, shake hands over it to indicate that they are in earnest and now what are we going to exchange—presents? What have you with you? My people expect presents in token of this friendship." The commanding officer then said that he would take these two men, Bear's Face and Long Feather, to his camp at the mouth of Tongue River and see what he could do. This officer didn't propose to take Sitting Bull's word, for he wanted Sitting Bull to deliver up a certain number of young men as hostages; that Sitting Bull might go and hunt buffalo and then come back; that if he didn't deliver up

Sitting Bull, Hunkpapa Lakota Leader in the Great Sioux War, ca. 1883. Photograph by David F. Barry. Courtesy of the Montana Historical Society.

hostages he should follow Sitting Bull. The officer said he was going into camp nearby and that Bear's Face and Long Feather could go with him and he would give them food. The commanding officer told Sitting Bull "to come with all his young men the next morning and have a talk with me. If you don't come to see me I shall go to see you."

In the morning Sitting Bull wanted to take his men to see this officer, but before he started the soldiers were discovered approaching the Indian camp in line of battle. So the Indians fled. [The informants stated] that Sitting Bull had declared that he had given his word that he should not fight the whites and that he would not break his word, and that he took all his men that he could get together and started to meet the soldiers in a peaceful manner; that they met and had another council again, but that at this council the officer told the Indians that he would open hostilities against them; that he should fight them (the interpreter on this occasion was John Brugher [Bruguier]; that the Indians went back to camp; the soldiers attacked them and killed one; that the Indians were still determined not to fight; that some fled in the direction of [Fort] Peck and some in the direction of Standing Rock Agency. The main body fled in this direction till they crossed the Little Missouri; that there Bear's Face and Long Feather, who had been with the Indians when attacked by the soldiers and accompanied the body which fled in the direction of Standing Rock, left this body of Indians. They heard after they left the camp that this officer said he had not done right by the Indians and he was again coming after them to renew his offers of peace. They heard that the officer made promises of food if the Indians would come and get it. He wanted them to come without reserve and get it. This was the last they heard.

They, Bear's Face and Long Feather, found at the place named, where the buffalo were tramped to death, two American horses; their own were used up; they

mounted these horses and rode them into the Indian
camp; that while there the Indians gave them two more
American horses; they started back with four horses with
the intention of turning them over to the commanding
officer, but they, one by one, were exhausted and abandoned. One only reached the neighborhood of Standing
Rock—it is probably dead by this time. They succeeded in
getting in with two Indian ponies each.

The following account by Spotted Elk, a Minneconjou Lakota,
supports the statement of Long Feather and Bear's Face. During
his life, Spotted Elk became revered more as a politician and
diplomat than a great warrior. In later life he played a central
role, under his name of Big Foot, in the Ghost Dance crisis that
preceded the tragedy at Wounded Knee. Spotted Elk's account of
Cedar Creek includes a description of the subsequent Yellow-
stone council and the surrender of some of the Sioux. It also
includes his impressions of the killing of five Sioux headmen by
Miles's Crow scouts on December 16, 1876, an event that likely
prolonged the Sioux War. The account is in Colonel W. H. Wood,
Eleventh U.S. Infantry, to Assistant Adjutant General, Depart-
ment of Dakota, March 1, 1877, in Nelson A. Miles Collection,
Folder: Indian Campaigns, 1877, U.S. Army Military History
Institute, Carlisle Barracks, Pennsylvania.

I LEFT THIS [CHEYENNE RIVER] AGENCY last fall with Bull
Eagle and several other Indians two days after I had had a
talk with the Commanding Officer here. The Indians
discovered at this talk that it was the intention of the
Government to disarm us and take our ponies away. Although he said nothing about taking them he kept asking
all the time how many we had. That made us think we were
going to be disarmed and dismounted. After we left here
we traveled night and day, throwing away our lodge poles
and other things to enable us to travel fast, until we
reached the Yellowstone, where we overtook the main
body of hostile Indians, and where we crossed that river
with them. We found there two Uncpapas, messengers

from Standing Rock Agency, who had been sent out on a friendly mission from the Commanding Officer of that post.

The day we crossed the Yellowstone we discovered troops, and these two messengers told us they would go with a flag of truce to them and get permission from the commander [Otis] for some of us to hold a parley with him. The Indians and troops by this time were drawn upon some hills facing each other. The two messengers went right in among the troops, and after a short time returned to a hill where all the head men had gathered. I was among that party. One of the messengers spoke and said: "The Commander wishes to see Sitting Bull and shake hands with him." Sitting Bull said he would not shake hands with him. This caused a great deal of dissatisfaction among those present. The other chiefs insisted that he should go. I, myself, told Sitting Bull that it was the desire of most of the Indians that he should go and shake hands with this officer, that I thought we could succeed in making a peace with him, and that we could then do it with more honor than we could hereafter. Sitting Bull then gave as his reason for not wanting to go that he was in mourning for the loss of a child who had just died. He said he was ashamed to go in the condition he was in to shake hands with anyone (the Indians, when they are in mourning, wear their worst clothes and look very bad). As Sitting Bull would not go, the two messengers with ten chiefs went to meet the officer, who gave them some rations after talking with them. He piled up the rations on the prairie and moved off and left them. The chiefs upon coming back abused Sitting Bull for not going to meet the officer when he was sent for. The officer we met had black whiskers, and was a large, heavy set man. We could not see his straps on account of his overcoat. I am sure he was not the officer the Indians call the "Man-with-the-Bear-Coat" [Miles]. We remained there in camp that day.

The next day we made a surround of buffalo, and
toward evening some spies whom we had out came in and
reported that troops were close by, coming down the north
bank of the Yellowstone. I mounted my horse and rode up a
hill from where I could see them. The Indians gathered
around me until there were several hundred watching the
troops approach. I told my people I did not want any of
them to attack the whites. While I was talking, Sitting Bull
and the two messengers came up. I proposed to Sitting
Bull and other chiefs that we should go, under a flag of
truce, and have a talk with the officer. They all consented.
We went to meet the officer and found him to be the "Man-
with-the-Bear-Coat," and shook hands with him.

The meeting took place in this way. The officer came
forward with an escort rolling cannon behind. The chiefs
approached with their young men following them. The
interpreter came out from among the troops and said the
Commander desired us to leave our young men behind, at
a reasonable distance, and meet him in the center. We told
him we would consent to that provided he would send back
his troops. It was done. Sitting Bull then took a robe,
spread it on the ground and invited the officer to sit down
on it. He refused to do so and they stood up and talked with
the robe spread out between them. Not much was said at
that time and we went back to camp. The interpreter of the
troops could not talk much; we could not understand very
well what he said. That night we tied up our horses. Some
of them getting loose, Indians went in search of them and
found the troops all around our camp. Many of the chiefs
were indignant at this and held a council of war. It was
proposed by many to attack the troops the next morning.
We finally agreed not to do so, but to be prepared for an
attack. No attack was made.

The next day, a party consisting of Sitting Bull, Black
Eagle, Bull Eagle, Rising Sun, Little Bear, Little White
Bull, Red Skirt, myself and others visited the Commander

of the troops. The "Man-with-the-Bear-Coat" approached us with a buffalo robe, spread it on the ground, and invited Sitting Bull to sit down on it. Sitting Bull would not do so, saying: "I spread a robe for you to sit on the other day and you refused. I shall have to refuse now to sit on your robe." This officer then invited the chiefs to sit down on it. I, with others, accepted. Sitting Bull seeing this sat down with us. The officer then sat down facing Sitting Bull, and shaking hands with him. Sitting Bull then filled a pipe and, presenting it to the Great Spirit, called upon Him to have mercy upon his people; to allow nothing to be said on either side but the truth; to look down upon them and influence the hearts of the Indians and whites so that they might do what is right in the council. He also said: "If any man of either party, who smokes this sacred pipe with me today, fails to keep his promises, I hope he may not live to walk upon the ground, but that he may lay down and die."

When he had said this he handed the pipe to the Man-with-the-Bear-Coat, who smoked and passed it to the chiefs, who all smoked in turn, Sitting Bull smoking last. The officer then invited all the Indians to go with him to the post at the mouth of Tongue River, and told them there would be a trading store there, and plenty of provisions to feed us all. Sitting Bull objected, saying "I prefer to remain on ground of my own selection and where there is plenty of game for my people. There is a trading store at Fort Peck where I do my trading and I propose to go there to do it."

All the talk on the part of the whites was holding out inducements for us to go with them to the mouth of Tongue River, and on the parts of the Indians refusing their offers. In this way the council broke up. We all started to return to our people, the troops following close behind us. The Interpreter overtook us and told us the troops were going to fire on us. Soon after, the firing commenced, and lasted until sundown. A brave young warrior and a good many of

Spotted Elk, Minneconjou Lakota, 1880s. Spotted Elk was later known as Chief Big Foot. He was killed at Wounded Knee in 1890. Courtesy of the Smithsonian Institution, National Anthropological Archives.

our horses were killed. We then broke camp and Sitting Bull, with a hundred lodges, went in the direction of Fort Peck. [Two days later] the others crossed to the south bank of the Yellowstone and again camped. The troops [who had pursued them] remained where they were on the north bank.

A young Indian, who returned to hunt for his horses, went into the camp of the troops. They shook hands with him, gave him something to eat and sent him away. When he got back he told Bull Eagle where he had been. The latter, with High Hawk (an uncle of the interpreter of the troops) then went to the camp of the troops. They remained there quite a while and were treated very kindly by the officer with the bear coat. They told each other a great many things. You ought to have heard them talk. You would have thought Bull Eagle was chief of all the Indians in the country, and the Man-with-the-Bear-Coat in command of all the whites. When Bull Eagle had got his belly full, the officer told him to select some of his head men and visit him in the morning. On returning to camp, Bull Eagle told the chiefs that the officer wanted to see them in the morning to make a treaty of peace with them. A council was held in our camp and we agreed what to do.

The next day a party of us went to the camp of the troops and there met the officer with the bear coat. He spread two blankets on the ground and we sat down on them. He then told us that he was having something cooked for us, that we could eat first and then talk. After our bellies were full our hearts got better. We asked him to give us several days to make a surround of buffalo and not to molest us with his troops; to have the Cheyenne [River] Agency moved to the fork of the Cheyenne and an army officer appointed as our agent in the place of a citizen; to give us rations enough to take us back to this agency, and to give us guns and ammunition. He made us many promises and we made many promises to him. I don't suppose he was able to fulfill all of his, and I know we were not able to fulfill all of ours.

One promise he made he did fulfill; this was to allow us five days to make a surround, and to give us one month's rations, provided we would agree to come to this agency and to give him five of our head men as hostages for the fulfillment of our part of the agreement. We then returned to camp, held a council and decided to do what he required of us. I learned, afterward, to my sorrow, that what the head men had decided upon in council was a trick played upon myself and others, who were in earnest, to gain time to make a surround, and to get the rations which we were very much in need of at that time.

The council selected five hostages and took them to the camp of the troops and delivered them to the Commander and received in return an immense pile of rations. None of the hostages were men of any importance. When I saw what men were selected by the council I began to suspect that they were playing a trick and would not go myself. I was asked to go. The men selected had always lived at this Agency and only left to save their horses. The Man-with-the-Bear-Coat gave us three papers, one of them to Bull Eagle, but did not read it to him. If he did, it was not interpreted to him, for he did not know what it said. The interpreter told us to show the papers to any troops or whites we met on the way in and they would not molest us. He also said, "When you arrive at Cheyenne Agency you will get all you have asked for." The troops then started toward the mouth of Tongue River, and we moved to Powder River. From this camp, Little Bear and some of the relations of the hostages stole away and came in here. Bull Eagle, with his wife and child, followed soon after.

There were in the main hostile camp at this time from five to six hundred lodges. Soon after we were joined by about three hundred lodges of Ogallalas and Cheyennes.

We then moved to Long Neck Creek on the Yellowstone, below the mouth of Tongue River. The post could be seen from the hills near our camp. While here small war parties from our camp were going and coming all the time, bringing back stolen property, which encouraged all the Indians.

One of these parties brought in some horses which they had stolen from the post above. When we found it out some of us chiefs proposed to take them back and return them to their owners. As some Indians had visited the post, got rations and been well treated, we were not afraid to go. Started with fourteen others, taking all the stolen horses, packed them with robes and furs, as we thought it would be a good opportunity to trade. On the way in we passed a party herding cattle from the post, and soon overtook a wood party with whom we rode along some distance. They seemed to know that we were friendly. We then rode ahead of them and I proposed to send, in advance, five of our party with a flag of truce, saying we would follow with the pack horses. This was done. Sitting Bull-the-Good, The Yearling, Fat Hide, Red Skirt No. 2, and Bad Leg took the flag and rode ahead. They were soon out of our sight and we heard firing. A great many shots were fired. Some one of our party said, "Our friends are being fired upon." We left our pack horses and ran back several hundred yards to a hill where we could get a better view. The firing had stopped, but we could see a great many people moving around in confusion, and could hear the war song of the Crow Indians. While on this hill a Sioux Indian came near enough to make himself heard and called us to come to him, but we were now afraid to go any closer and he appeared to be afraid to come to us. We did not see those men killed. We thought they had been and, leaving all the horses and packs, we returned to camp. Our only object in going to the Post was a friendly mission to return those horses.

Lazy White Bull gave additional details of the conferences between the Sioux and Miles at Cedar Creek in an interview with Walter M. Camp on July 23, 1910, interpreter unknown. White Bull's reminiscence is in Walter Camp Interview Notes, Manuscript 57, Box 2, Walter M. Camp Collection, Archives and Manuscripts, Harold B. Lee Library, Brigham Young University, Provo, Utah.

GEN. MILES AND THREE SOLDIERS. Sitting Bull, Lazy White Bull, High Bear, and Little Bear. High Bear took a buffalo robe and spread [it] down for Gen. Miles to sit on, but Miles knelt on it and would not sit on it. John Bruguier . . . was interpreter.

Gen. Miles' troops had scared away a herd of buffalo that Sioux were after and the Sioux had taken 60 head of mules from Miles. Miles said he wanted the mules back and Sitting Bull said, "Give us back the buffalo your soldiers scared away from us."

The next morning they met again and Miles asked Sitting Bull if he was determined to fight white people. Sitting Bull said no, but said, "You white people are making guns and shells to fight Indians with and every chance you get you attack our camps. That's the reason we have to fight."

Gen. Miles said, "If you want to make a settlement I can be reached." Sitting Bull said, "I want to make my home in the Black Hills. I have always tried to be a decent Indian, but every time your soldiers come around they start shooting us."

After this Gen. Miles went back and the fight commenced and [they] killed a son of Bad Hair (Hunkpapa).

Chapter 9
The Dull Knife Battle, November 25, 1876

Iron Teeth, Black White Man, Beaver Heart, and Various Other Northern Cheyennes

In the aftermath of the Little Big Horn battle, most of the Northern Cheyennes traveled south, seeking familiar recesses along the headwaters of the Tongue and Powder rivers in Wyoming Territory. As winter approached, the followers of chiefs Dull Knife and Little Wolf found shelter and security from the soldiers along tributaries in the Big Horn Mountains. While Miles continued his operations along the Yellowstone, Crook's army again took the field, and on November 25 his cavalry, commanded by Colonel Ranald S. Mackenzie, discovered Dull Knife's village and launched a dawn attack. The battle proved to be one of the largest engagements in the war and effectively ended Northern Cheyenne participation in the conflict. Surviving Cheyennes fled north to find succor with Crazy Horse's Oglalas in Montana; other gravitated toward the agencies and eventually surrendered.

Reminiscent Cheyenne testimony of the Dull Knife battle is provided in four statements. That of the Northern Cheyenne woman, Iron Teeth, was taken by Thomas B. Marquis in 1929, when she was ninety-five years old. Her account presents a noncombatant perspective on the fighting and something of a context in describing events immediately preceding and following the battle. It is excerpted from Marquis, "Red Ripe's Squaw," Century Magazine 118 (June 1929).

IN THE MIDDLE OF THE SUMMER we heard that all of the soldiers had been killed at the Little Bighorn River. . . . My husband said we should [leave Red Cloud Agency and] go and join our people there. We went, and all of our people spent the remainder of the summer there [Mon-

tana], hunting, not bothering any white people nor wanting to see any of them. When the leaves fell, the Cheyenne
camp was located on a small creek far up the Powder River.
Soldiers came (November 25, 1876) and fought us
there. Crows, Pawnees, Shoshones, some Arapahoes and
other Indians were with them. They killed our men,
women and children, whichever ones might be hit by their
bullets. We who could do so ran away. My husband and my
two sons helped in fighting off the soldiers and enemy
Indians. My husband was walking, leading his horse, and
stopping at times to shoot. Suddenly, I saw him fall. I
started to go back to him, but my sons made me go on, with
my three daughters. The last time I ever saw Red Ripe, he
was lying there dead in the snow. From the hilltops we
Cheyennes saw our lodges and everything in them burned.

We wallowed through the mountain snows for several
days. Most of us were afoot. We had no lodges, only a few
blankets, and there was only a little dry meat food among
us. Men died of wounds, women and children froze to
death. After eleven days of this kind of traveling we found a
camp of Oglala Sioux. They fed us, but the rest of that
winter was a hard one for all of us.

*The following narrative integrates the recollections of several
Cheyennes interviewed by George Bird Grinnell during a tour
of the Dull Knife battlefield on June 30, 1916. It reposes in Field
Notebook 354 of the Grinnell Collection, Braun Research Library, Southwest Museum, Los Angeles.*

THE TROOPS CAME in from east up creek. Hairy Hand says
they heard the shooting a long way down the creek, but
this is probably wrong, for the soldiers charging the village
would not be shooting off guns in the air at nothing.
Fisher's widow, the aunt-in-law of Willis [Rowland], says
the shooting did not begin until troops or scouts were
almost at village. The men with me [Grinnell] said that
Crow Splitnose warned the camp shortly that soldiers

Iron Teeth, Northern Cheyenne, at age ninety-three. Courtesy of the Montana Historical Society.

were coming, but women say it was a man named Meat. The camp began about opposite the red butte on north side of stream and near it, and extended up the stream. The lodge occupied by Willis' aunt was close under the clump of box elders still standing on south side of stream.

Nshka after she was lost by family set out to run toward the breastworks on north side of river and well up toward head of a little wash and in open plain. As she was running a young man charged down and called to her to turn to her left and run up the stream. He passed her and then turned apparently intending to run by her to pick her up and carry her to safety, but just then her father, Elk River, who was looking for her, came along and took her in charge.

Braided Locks who early in the fight was shot through the body turned to walk away to shelter and as he went the balls fell so thickly about him that to him "it seemed as if I was walking on bullets."

Hairy Hand was fighting with a friend and the soldiers got close so that they had to retreat. Just as they started the friend was shot through the leg just below the knee and fell. Hairy Hand went on a hundred yards and then thought that he must not leave his friend there. He turned and ran back and carried his friend away. He did not carry him all the way on his back for the man could hop along a little on his good leg while the other leg swung free.

Crow Split Nose was killed just about where the road passes along under the foot of the butte on which the Shoshoni scouts were—south side of stream—but the stone put there by Cheyennes to mark the place has been moved. His body was rescued by Dog Hotam e wi (the dog said—or perhaps spoke). When they first charged up to take it away the fire was so hot that they could not take it. They did, however, put about it a blanket they had brought. This wrapping in a blanket seems to be part of a burial ceremony. Ask as to this. [Marginal note: no] The firing at these men was not from the scouts on the red butte above them—Shoshoni—for the Cheyennes were so close under the bluff as to be out of sight of these men. It must have come from some other group of troops across the creek. The second time Dog and his men rushed up to take the body they were successful and carried the man off. . . .

Little Wolf and Dull Knife, Northern Cheyenne leaders in the Great Sioux War. Photograph by Alexander Gardner, 1873. Courtesy of the Nebraska State Historical Society.

After getting an idea of the field from the high points, we went down to the valley and after meeting Mrs. Graves whose ranch is on the battle field, we crossed the creek and walked over the field. We saw where Lt. McKinney fell, where Bull Hump fought, where Long Jaw was cornered and was helped out by the 20 men in war bonnets, and where 6 young men were killed close under the mountain. Braided Locks had a friend among these young men who were killed after fighting for some time behind a cedar tree. Braided Locks went over there to see if he could find the tree but found only the stump. It has been cut down for fence post.

Dog and a friend were fighting from a certain point near northwest corner of the valley and Dog went there to find some of his shells if he could. He found none but did find one or two of those fired by his friend. These were rather long .35 caliber and of brass. Was there not a Winchester of this size made about that time?

Different members of the party must have picked up 40 or 50 cartridge shells, many of copper and some of brass. Most were centre fire but without a primer. One short rim fire shell looked like an old 14 gr. .44 Henry rifle. One unused shell had a primer in it. It was a Springfield carbine cartridge, I think. Some of these shells might be shown to Winchester company's expert or to experts at Frankford, Pa. arsenal.

At the upper—west—end of valley the stream forks and it was up the northwest branch which flows through a deep narrow canon that the women and children fled. As soon as they had turned to the right and got out of range of the bullets, the women stopped and climbed up to the easterly brink of the canon and there began to build breastworks. They seem to have feared that the large body of troops, whites, and Indians intended to follow them up and exterminate them. They therefore made preparations to fight every foot of the way, and it is not likely that they could ever have been driven from this position. At all events they made ready to fight, but during the night retreated up the mountain side. On a high grassy slope between the forks of the creek, southwest of where women retreated to, there were a large number of horses feeding that had not been disturbed by the battle. They remained here, and a few days later some of the Cheyennes returned and recovered all the horses.

The women say there greatest suffering of the fight was the climbing the mountain at night. A man led each group of women and children that struggled up the steep ascent.

The account by Beaver Heart, Cheyenne, was given in 1934 at the dedication of a Daughters of the American Revolution (DAR) marker on the Rosebud battlefield. Beaver Heart was nineteen years old at the time of the Dull Knife battle. His account is excerpted from an unpublished typescript, "They Fought Crook and Custer," by Jack Keenan, Miscellaneous Articles, Wyoming Work Projects Administration, Wyoming State Archives and Historical Department, Cheyenne.

"[WE LEARNED] AHEAD OF TIME that soldiers were coming," recalled old Beaver Heart. "Many people meant to go into mountains. Fox soldier chief, Last Bull (the man charged with defending the camp), say, 'No, we stay here.' So we stayed." In the light of later events, this was a tactical error. The camp knew Mackenzie's column was coming up the stream. Yet, strangely, the Indians spent the night of November 25 [November 24] dancing. It was nearly dawn when they broke up and went to bed.

Gray light was seeping into the canyon when the charge came. The thunder of hoofs and the war chants of enemy scouts awoke the village. Rifles and pistols took up their song of death.

"I rush from my lodge," Beaver Heart is signing. "I am naked. It is very cold. I run for my life. Soldiers everywhere. There is no time to snatch up even a robe. Pawnees and Shoshonis shoot at me. I run faster up the canyon toward the mountainside. Many of my people dead. Others run with me."

The story of that rout will live as long as red children listen to old men's tales around gleaming camp fires.

Beaver Heart's account jibes with written history. He probably was in the lower end of the camp when the attack was launched. The Cheyennes' heaviest loss was suffered here as the Pawnee scouts poured deadly volleys into teepees, killing without discretion all whom they contacted. A few of the warriors in the upper end of the village had time to buckle on cartridge belts and seize their guns. These organized a resistance and held off the invaders until women and children got to improvised breastworks on the mountainside. There the fight continued until darkness and then began a retreat as heroic as any in history.

Cut off from their horse herds, their village in smoking ruins, without food and burdened with women, children and their wounded, these red soldiers eluded their pursuers and marched for three days before they got help.

Even as he spoke, shadows came into Beaver Heart's eyes. Those were terrible days. The nights were alive with the cries of men tortured with wounds and women and children dying of cold. During the fighting at the village, Two Moons the younger sneaked into a lodge and picked up three buffalo robes. These were the only coverings for the women and their little ones. Gravely, Beaver Heart recalled how children were warmed back to life by stuffing them into the stomachs of butchered horses.

On the first morning three of the fugitives ran off some Pawnee scouts and recovered about 75 head of their horses. Without these the party probably would have perished. There was no food except horse meat. Cooking utensils had been left behind and destroyed by the soldiers. The meat had to be roasted on beds of coals while sentries watched against fresh attacks.

Many white authorities of such standing as Major North, commander of Pawnee scouts, say the Indians went down the Powder river to the camp of Crazy Horse. Beaver Heart, and his account fits in with Grinnell's [*The Fighting Cheyennes*], has a different version. He claims the band followed the ridges of the Big Horn [Mountains] until they reached Lodge Pole creek. They went down this stream to a lake and then crossed to Prairie Dog, or Crow Stand Creek, and followed that to the Tongue River. Here, freezing and half starved, they were found by Crazy Horse's scouts and brought to the Sioux chieftain's village on the Tongue.

The account of Black White Man, who was thirty-one years old in 1876, was given to George Bird Grinnell in 1908. It is in Item 91, "Mackenzie's Fight and Cheyenne War Miscellany," in the Grinnell Collection, Braun Research Library, Southwest Museum, Los Angeles.

BLACK WHITE MAN was in Dull Knife's village in 1876 when it was captured. His son, a boy, had then returned from a war party against the Snakes shot in the buttocks, the ball coming out through the right thigh.

When the troops charged the village that morning the balls hitting the lodges sounded like hail-stones. Black White Man was obliged to saddle the horse for his wife and son. He put his boy on a horse and told the two to ride away while he ran toward the troops. When he reached a little ridge and looked over he could see the soldiers on the other slope of the ridge crawling up toward the top on their bellies. The Indians fired at them and the soldiers fell back a little. He turned about and looked back at the village and there in front of his lodge, which stood close to the river, he saw a number of his horses that he had tied up the night

Pictographic Drawing by the seventy-three-year-old Northern Cheyenne, Limpy, in 1930, showing the Army Attack on Dull Knife's Village in November 1876, and the Battle of Rosebud Creek on the previous June 17. Dr. Thomas B. Marquis's accompanying comments: "Use your imagination to supply omitted details. At upper right, the human figure represents about 1,500 soldiers. Three Indians on horseback, one standing, and two lying down, represent the six different tribes—Osage, Pawnee, Shoshone, Arapaho, Crow, and Sioux—having about 400 of their warriors accompanying the soldiers as helpers. The few Cheyennes shown in flight afoot represent about 1,700 in camp. The few tepees represent the whole tribal camp. Horse tracks at upper right show Cheyenne horse herd driven away. The one discarded buffalo robe

stands for many such articles and other property discarded in the flight, most of it left in tepees. Short pencil dashes indicate footprints of fleeing Cheyennes. Pencil dashes having nub-ends indicate bullets flying. Cheyenne men are fighting back. Women and children were not spared by the attackers, so they are running away—if they can. Limpy, at left of tepee group, had neither weapon nor horse. His footprints show where he had tried to get a horse from the herd, but failed. Limpy's wife, upper left, wearing buffalo horns. She was shot through the chest, front to back. Observe her wound, her coughing up blood, and her bloody trail. I examined, in 1929 and 1930, the scars of that wound. Upper center, blind old man, carrying pipe, killed. Note his wound. A surprise attack. The Cheyennes, all afoot, walked through snow of the Bighorn Mountains to Tongue River. Down that river to Ogallala Sioux camp. Eleven days of such travel. Many starved or froze to death. Nov.-Dec. 1876.

Lower segment depicts Rosebud battle, June 17, 1876, against Gen. Crook, with Crow and Shoshone allies. Limpy's horse was killed by Crow-Shoshone enemies. He hid behind a big stone and fought off those warriors. He had only a six-shooter, they had rifles. Many bullets and arrows flying, many horse tracks, all indicate much activity there at that time. Use your imagination. Observe the string of beads Limpy is wearing. They are the same I obtained from him in August, 1930, now in my Custer battle museum." Courtesy of Little Bighorn Battlefield National Monument.

before running back and forth trying to break their ropes. He ran back to his lodge to cut the ropes and then on foot drove the horses toward the breastworks. On his way he overtook a little boy running toward the breastworks and went on with him, in front and even between his legs, but neither he nor the little boy were hit. He cannot explain how it was. At length they reached the breastworks.

Chapter 10
The Battle of Wolf Mountains,
January 8, 1877
Eagle Shield, Oglala Lakota; and Wooden Leg,
Northern Cheyenne

The surrender that Colonel Miles negotiated with the Sioux following the councils and fighting at Cedar Creek proved inconclusive; of the approximately two thousand people who agreed to terms along the Yellowstone, only a few dozen actually turned themselves in at the Dakota agencies. Most stayed in the field and joined Crazy Horse and other leaders south of the Yellowstone.

Sitting Bull continued to elude the troops. In early November, Miles and his infantrymen departed the Tongue River Cantonment to seek out the Hunkpapa chief and his followers. The soldiers trailed the Indians north to the Fort Peck Indian Agency on the Missouri River, then headed west in a fruitless chase that fatigued the command before they returned to the winter garrison in December. A battalion of Miles's infantry, detached under First Lieutenant Frank D. Baldwin on December 2, overtook Sitting Bull five days later as the tribesmen forded the frozen Missouri east of Fort Peck. The soldiers skirmished briefly with the Lakotas before returning to Fort Peck for provisions.

On December 18, Baldwin located Sitting Bull's village of 122 lodges along Ash Creek, a tributary of Redwater River south of the Missouri. Many of the warriors were away hunting. Baldwin attacked at midday, pursuing the occupants into the cold and capturing the village and its contents before returning to the cantonment. The army victory proved costly to the Sioux, and Sitting Bull's remaining influence within the native coalition quickly ebbed; over the next several months most of his people crossed the international boundary to Canada. No Indian accounts of Baldwin's fights on December 7 and 18 are known to exist.

Meantime, active raiding by warriors in the vicinity of the cantonment focused Miles's attention south of the Yellowstone. On December 31 he set forth with his troops to locate Crazy Horse's people, augmented now by the arrival of the Cheyenne refugees from Dull Knife's village. These Indians occupied an encampment near the mouth of Hanging Woman Creek on the upper Tongue. Early in January, Miles's scouts captured a party of women and children en route to the village. On January 8, in an effort to rescue their kin, several hundred Sioux and Cheyennes attacked the army bivouac along Tongue River, precipitating a major engagement that lasted several hours until a rising blizzard quelled the fighting. At the Battle of Wolf Mountains, the Indians held the lofty buttes and ridges south of the river; Miles's command, clad in buffalo greatcoats and fur caps, physically wrested the heights from the warriors. Both sides suffered under the extreme weather conditions.

Two accounts of Wolf Mountains follow. That of Eagle Shield, while brief, offers an Oglala perspective given within a few weeks of the event. Eagle Shield was approximately twenty-one years old in 1877. His testimony is in Lieutenant Colonel George P. Buell to the Assistant Adjutant General, Department of Dakota, February 19, 1877, National Archives, Record Group 393 (Records of United States Army Continental Commands, 1821–1920), Item 1249.

I HAVE THE HONOR to inform you that after sending off my report of the 16th instant, containing the statement made to me by Eagle Shield, the mail arrived here bringing the news of a recent fight between the troops and Indians on Tongue River [in the Wolf Mountains]. During the day it occurred to me that Eagle Shield, in answering the question as to whether there had been any fighting between the Indians and troops since the fight with the Cheyennes, might have referred to the last fight [Wolf Mountains], while I had in my mind when asking the question, the fight in November last [with Dull Knife's people]. I caused him to be brought before me again, and through the interpreter said: "The other day I asked you if there had been any

Eagle Shield, Oglala Lakota, in 1913. Photograph by Frances
Densmore. Courtesy of the South Dakota State Archives.

fight between the troops and Indians since the fight with
the Cheyennes. You replied 'No!' Now when did that fight
with the Cheyennes occur?" He then asked, "Which fight
do you mean? The one with the troops from Red Cloud
Agency?" I answered, "No! I mean has there been any

recent fight?" At first he said, "No!" Then, after hesitating for some time, and after being assured that he had nothing to fear by telling the truth, he answered: "There was a fight on Tongue River, near the mouth of Suicide Creek,[12] just before the old moon went out, ten days before I left." (He left about the 17th of January.)

Upon being asked to tell all he knew about that fight, he stated as follows:

"There was a party of Cheyennes out from the main camp, hunting buffalo, seven lodges. The main camp was then between the present camp on Prairie Dog Creek, and Suicide Creek. The party had finished their hunt and were returning to the main camp, and on the way back the men had become separated from the women, from some cause or other, when the latter, seven of them, are supposed to have come in sight of a camp which they mistook for the main hostile camp, thinking it had been moved during their absence. They were captured [by the troops]. The men following shortly after discovered what had happened, returned to the main camp and reported what had occurred. A war party, consisting mainly of Cheyennes and Ogallalas, was then formed and went down the river, attacked the troops and drove them back. Three Indians were wounded, one in the leg, one in the neck, and the other in the left side. Two Indians were killed, one Runs-the-Bear, a Sioux from this Agency, the other a Cheyenne, whose name I don't know. The fight occurred in the afternoon and lasted until night.[13] The Indians then stopped and waited all the next day, and the day after until noon, when the soldiers left and did not come back any more. Crazy Horse, head chief of the Ogallalas led the fight. Only a portion of the war party raised went, about four hundred. A great many did not go because they wanted the soldiers to come up and fight them at the main camp, in the rough country. I was in the fight. The troops did not follow us up at all. It was three days from the time the soldiers captured the women until they went back. When the fight began, the troops marched up first in line, and then spread out. There were about a thousand of them.[14] We did not think there were any soldiers killed, as we went to their camp-ground after the fight was over, and could find no sign of any having been buried. We expected to be followed up and attacked by the soldiers. . . . "

The reminiscent account of Wooden Leg provides details of the battle from the Northern Cheyenne viewpoint. It was given in the 1920s to Thomas B. Marquis. The account is excerpted from Marquis, A Warrior Who Fought Custer (Minneapolis: Midwest Company, 1931).

AFTER WE HAD RESTED with the Ogallalas a few days the chiefs counciled together and decided that the tribes should join in movement up the Tongue river. All of us then followed our back trail over to Otter creek and on to Tongue river. We moved slowly and hunted along the way. The Cheyennes got a new supply of buffalo meat and many more skins for enlarging their lodges. We crossed Tongue river on the ice, to the east side. Not far up the valley we went back over the ice, to the west side. We traveled then on up the benchland trails, to Hanging Woman creek. The Ogallalas had some cattle they had taken from white people or from soldiers. These were butchered along the way. They had yet also a few of the horses taken at the battle on the Little Bighorn. But these horses that had been so fat and strong were now poor and weak. Most of them already had died. They did not know how to find winter food like the Indian ponies could find it.

At Hanging Woman creek it was decided the two tribes would separate. The Ogallalas would go eastward up this stream. The Cheyennes would continue on up Tongue river valley. As usual, a few Cheyennes joined the Sioux and a few of their people decided to come with us. My

sister Crooked Nose started with the other people. Chiefs
Crazy Horse and Water All Gone and a few other Ogallalas
came to us. Just as the tribes were about to separate, some
scouts brought in the report:

"Soldiers are coming!"

The two bands of Indians began to come again together. The warriors mingled themselves as being of one tribe.
The women and children and older men of both sets of
people moved together up the Tongue river. The young
men put themselves behind their fleeing people. Somebody said to me:

"They have captured some women. Your sister is one
of them."

My heart jumped when this news came to me. I
lashed my horse into a run toward where it was said they
had been captured. There I saw tracks of soldier horses.
The trail led to the river ice. On the opposite side of the
river, the west side, were soldiers. They began shooting at
me. I had to get away. I did not see any of the women, so I
supposed they had been killed. My heart then became
bitter toward these white men.

I hid my horse in the brush at the foot of a ridge where
some warriors were on its top. I walked up there. Many
Indians were hidden behind rocks and were shooting
toward the soldiers. I chose for myself a hiding place and
did the same. I had my soldier rifle and plenty of cartridges. Many soldiers were coming across on the ice, to
fight us. But we had the advantage of them because of our
position on the high and rocky ridge.

Big Crow, a Cheyenne, kept walking back and forth
along the ridge on the side toward the soldiers.[15] He was
wearing a warbonnet. He had a gun taken from the soldiers
at the Little Bighorn battle. He used up his cartridges and
came back to us hidden behind the rocks, to ask for more.
Cheyennes and Sioux here and there each gave him one or
two or three. He soon got enough to fill his belt. He went

out again to walk along the ridge, to shoot at the soldiers and to defy them in their efforts to hit him with a bullet. All of us others kept behind the rocks, only peeping around at times to shoot. Crazy Horse, the Ogallala chief, was near me. Bullets glanced off the shielding rocks, but none hit us. One came close to me. It whizzed through the folds of my blanket at my side.

Big Crow finally dropped down. He lay there alive, but apparently in great distress. A Sioux went with me to crawl down to where he was and bring him into shelter. Another Sioux came after us. When we got to the wounded man I took hold of his feet and the two Sioux grasped his hands. The three of us crawled and dragged him along on the snow. Bullets began to shower around us. We let loose our holds and dodged behind rocks. When the firing quieted, we crept out and again got him. My brother just then called out to me: "Wooden Leg, come, we are going away from here." I let loose again and went to my brother. The two Sioux continued to drag Big Crow.

The Indians moved back and forth, down and up, fighting the soldiers at different times all day. After darkness came, the fighting stopped. The group where I was built a little fire, so we might warm ourselves. As soon as the light of it showed, the bullets began to sing over our heads. We quickly threw snow upon the fire. Then we moved to another place. I got down where I had left my horse. It was still there. I mounted and joined my friends. All of the Indians left there during the night. Some of the Ogallalas already had gone on up Hanging Woman creek. Chiefs Crazy Horse and Water All Gone, with many lodges of their people, attached themselves to the Cheyennes. We went up Tongue river. We traveled all night and all the next day before we stopped to camp.

We did not know where these soldiers had come from. We did not know either how far they might follow us. But our scouts remaining behind saw them go back down

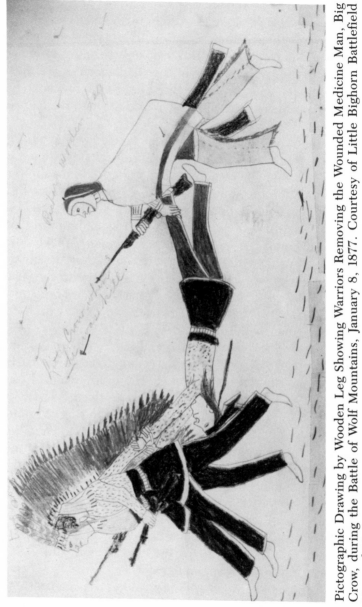

Pictographic Drawing by Wooden Leg Showing Warriors Removing the Wounded Medicine Man, Big Crow, during the Battle of Wolf Mountains, January 8, 1877. Courtesy of Little Bighorn Battlefield National Monument.

Tongue river. At the camp, Big Crow's relatives went about inquiring for him. I told where I last had seen him. Finally, they found the two Sioux who had been with him when I left him. These men said he was dead. That was our one man lost in the battle. Two Sioux were killed.

Chapter 11
The Lame Deer Fight,
May 7, 1877
White Bull, Northern Cheyenne, and Hump, Minneconjou Lakota

The Wolf Mountains Battle represented a major watershed in the Sioux War by signaling to the remaining Sioux and Cheyennes the reality of their waning fortunes. Now destitute, starving, weakened by the unyielding force of winter, and faced with the unremitting military power of the U.S. government, the people of Crazy Horse, Two Moon, and the other tribal leaders deliberated over their future. In the late winter and early spring, following initiatives from both Miles and emissaries from the Nebraska agencies, the Indians started to surrender. In March, three hundred Cheyennes and a few Lakotas turned themselves in at the cantonment. Hundreds more, including Crazy Horse, gave up at Camp Robinson, Nebraska.

One group of Lakotas, Minneconjous headed by Lame Deer, chose to prolong their independence, attracting to them some Cheyennes of like intent. By early May, these people occupied a village along Muddy Creek near Rosebud Creek. On May 7, Miles's soldiers attacked the camp, chasing men, women, and children into the adjoining hills and killing Lame Deer and several of his followers. The action was the last major confrontation in the war.

The accounts below comprise reminiscent testimony of two men, Cheyenne and Lakota, who accompanied Colonel Miles's troops in the attack on Lame Deer's camp. Both had become scouts for Miles, and their accounts provide a unique perspective of surrendered warriors who were obliged to serve their former enemies. White Bull, also known as Ice, a respected leader and medicine man among the Northern Cheyennes, took a prominent part in the events of 1876–77. Faced with hopelessness as he watched his people suffer through the winter, White Bull led them into the cantonment in March, then enlisted as a scout for Miles and guided him to Lame Deer's camp. He provided two accounts of the army attack in interviews with George Bird Grinnell in 1900 and 1906. The first is in Field Notebook 333, the Grinnell Collection, Braun Research Library, Southwest Museum, Los Angeles.

GEN. MILES AND SCOUTS left Ft. Keogh.[16] Brave Wolf and White Bull and John Bruguier were sent on ahead after they struck Rosebud. Lame Deer had come down Tongue River and crossed to Rosebud and camped at mouth of Lame Deer [Muddy Creek]. . . . Gen. Miles sent for him and told him that he had heard that there were people up above mouth of Rosebud and to choose a man and find out who they were. He chose Brave Wolf. The first day they left, came up Tongue River and camped at Pumpkin Creek [and] troops were there. Next camp on Tongue River. Next on Tongue River. Gen. Miles told him to go out and look up people. He [White Bull] took another man and pack train mules up Tongue River, struck trail and followed it over to the Rosebud and found where they [the Minneconjous] had camped. After finding this he went onto a high hill and decided that they must be camped on Rosebud or Lame Deer. He went back to soldiers camp on Tongue River, reaching there at dark. He reported where he had been and what he had found. He told Gen. Miles that he could look down on Rosebud and see buffalo moving off and thought it must be camped in here somewhere.

It was getting late in the day. Gen. Miles went out and looked about and asked White Bull if he thought he could reach where they had been camped by day next morning. White Bull said he thought so and they started, leaving wagons behind. At sundown they reached Rosebud and at day light reached the old camp where White Bull had been before. Some infantry and some cavalry got there. Gen. Miles told him to go on and see what he could find and to take an interpreter with him. He gave him a good horse that could run fast and told him if he got in to close quarters to let him run and to get back to camp same night.

They started and struck Rosebud below mouth of Lame Deer, crossed it and came up. He left interpreter down below and climbed conical hill back of [where] slaughter pen [stood in 1900 in later community of Lame Deer]. From there he saw the camp and got the lay of country. He went back to interpreter and found him standing in a low place. He told White Bull to look up the creek and when he did so he saw a lot of Indians who had been hunting buffalo coming back with loads of meat. They crossed the hills toward the camp. White Bull and interpreter went down Rosebud. When near where they thought camp was, interpreter blew a whistle that he had and at last got an answer. When they got back to camp went to Gen. Miles tent and told him what he had seen and where Indians were camped.

That night they started travelling slow so as to reach camp about daylight. When they came to the high hill they stopped and took Gen. Miles onto it to show him where the camp was. As soon as he saw it he went down and went back and met command where they were down below by water. They saw an Indian come up over the hill. He went back to camp but did not notify camp but himself with family packed up and went off. Gen. Miles sent two scouts up near to camp. They came within sight and one of them came back and reported that the camp was quiet, no one moving about. They came up creek on a trot but up above there they made the charge, passing through a point in the stream and some horses fell with soldiers. The first shot was fired where the dance house stands [in 1900]. You could see the Indian horses stampeded in all directions and women and children running up the hills on foot to take refuge among the pines. It was not good daylight.

While the fighting was going on there were Indians in the creek bed fighting. With Gen. Miles was a Indian scout

White Bull, Northern Cheyenne, late 1880s. Photograph by Christian Barthelmess. Courtesy of the Smithsonian Institution, National Anthropological Archives.

named Hump. He started down to these Indians calling out and presently Indians stopped shooting and Gen. Miles ordered firing to cease. Then Lame Deer and some others came up out of creek. Hump came to Gen. Miles and told him that Lame Deer wanted to see him and make peace with him. Miles called an officer and went down to where Lame Deer was. He told them to put their firearms down and Lame Deer put his down. Miles told them they must surrender their guns and horses and would be taken back to Keogh. Lame Deer's son had a warbonnet on.

When Lame Deer put down his gun [it] was full cocked. The Indian said, "I am a soldier. I will give up my gun to no one. They have already killed my grandmother." They had killed an old woman. White Bull rode up to Lame Deer's son and took hold of his gun to take it away and the officer took hold of his arm but he wouldn't give up the gun. Lame Deer tried to pursuade the boy to give it up but he would not. Then Lame Deer said, "All right son," and ran to his gun and caught it up and shot at Gen. Miles. Lame Deer's son tried to shoot White Bull but he pushed muzzle away. A soldier ran up and shot at son but missed and killed a soldier. After they shot, Lame Deer and son ran down to creek but when they got there son was dragging his gun by the muzzle as if weak and his father took him by the shoulder as if to help him. Then somebody began to shoot and all fell. When they rushed up son raised up but he was weak and [the scout] Bob Jackson shot him in the head.

The pack train was behind with ammunition. Some Sioux went around through hills [and] killed one man and the riding mule of the other who fought his way up the creek on foot. Sioux got all ammunition. They [the soldiers] fought all day and next day went back and destroyed camp.

Lame Deer was not lame. The son was his nephew whom he had raised. His father was Wind, Lame Deer's brother. There were about 30 lodges.

White Bull's 1906 account, which offers additional details, is in Notebook 345, Grinnell Collection, Braun Research Library, Southwest Museum, Los Angeles.

MILES SENT FOR WHITE BULL saying white people have reported that somebody is chasing buffalo at mouth of Rosebud. I think it may be Indians. Go and find out. White Bull went to Brave Wolf and said I am going out, enlist as a scout and go with me. Brave Wolf did so. They went out with Miles and his orderly, the troops having moved out the day before, and came as far as the big bend of Rosebud and camped on Tongue River. Next morning Gen. Miles sent interpreter and White Bull out on scout. The two went out to look for trail, crossed the Rosebud and went some distance and struck a trail. Same day troops moved over to Rosebud. White Bull and interpreter followed trail to Indian camp where they found fresh meat thrown out that had not had time to spoil. They followed trail a little way till it turned back to Rosebud and struck it below mouth of Lame Deer below the Painted Rocks. When they got there they saw the soldiers coming. They stopped there until they came up. White Bull had been out one night, but troops [had been out] two for they left day before Gen. Miles.

When he [White Bull] met soldiers, Gen. Miles sent him on to follow trail until he saw something, saying that troops would remain here till his return. He and interpreter set out on trail which crossed Rosebud at mouth of Lame Deer. When they got to mouth of Lame Deer it was still light but sun was low. They went up on point south of Lame Deer to look up Rosebud. When they looked up there they saw a long string of Indians coming in from the buffalo chase with loaded horses crossing over the trail where the wagon road now goes. When they saw this they pulled back their horses to hide in the ravines until these people should have got out of sight.

When the people had disappeared, White Bull and interpreter went up through the hills and crossed the trail of the buffalo hunters where the road runs now [1906] and where there used to be water [in 1877]. When they got there, they drank and rode up on the hills a little and both got off their horses. White Bull said both of us cannot leave the horses. One must stay and hold them while the other climbs that hill to look. If we leave them someone may take our horses away. Interpreter said, "You go." He gave him a little book and pencil and said to him, "Take this and any time you see a lodge make a mark and when you get back I will add it up for you."

White Bull climbed the hill and looked over and saw the camp. He counted up to 10 and made a mark in the book. He counted all the lodges he could see and when the interpreter counted them he made 38 lodges. It was springtime but the grass was up well. . . . He returned and handed the interpreter his book and pencil. Interpreter said, "Wait. I will write a note about this." They started back to troops. By this time they had got to mouth of Lame Deer. It was quite dark. They could see nothing but they knew where they had left the troops at the Painted Rocks.

When they came close to the troops, the interpreter took out a little whistle that he had and he took out the whistle and blew it. This was an understood signal and when the sentry heard it he would know who it was and would call out to them. When they got in camp they reported to Gen. Miles where the camp was and how far off. Interpreter had made notes of position of camp. Gen. Miles said, "You better get something to eat first." After they had eaten, Gen. Miles sent for White Bull and said, "White Bull, what do you think about our starting tonight? Did you get the lay of country and see whether we can get the troops in?" "Yes," White Bull said. "Right up that creek is a red point. I think that will be a good place to put the troops tonight. It is near the camp." (This point is nearly a mile below agency [in 1906].) They started and stopped for the night at this red point.

Just before daylight, White Bull went to top of hill and saw lights in some of the lodges. The women had begun to build their fires. Thought it was not yet good daylight. He returned to soldiers and asked Gen. Miles if he would not walk up to the top of a little hill and look at the camp. They did so and saw part of camp and some lights in the lodges. Gen. Miles spoke to his orderly, who rode back to the command and Gen. Miles and White Bull followed. No noise was made. Word was passed among the soldiers and all got ready. There was some cavalry and some infantry. A cavalry horse was led up to him and given him and his pony taken. (He had been riding it for two days now.) He spoke to interpreter and said, "Tell Gen. Miles I have another idea in my head and I think we can work it so that before they know anything about it we will be around them. When I was on the hill yesterday I saw two little creeks coming in, one at the camp and one just below it. On the hill on the other side the [Indian camp] there are pine trees. I can take the cavalry up to the first creek I saw and take them up that and over the divide and down the other and on the other side I can take the cavalry up and get above them and the infantry can go up the main valley here." "No," said the interpreter, "Let us give these poor people a chance to get away." "But," said White Bull, "if we surround them they will have to surrender and we will get them all." But the interpreter said no and did not speak to Gen. Miles.

The troops started, they got nearly up to where agency now stands. They saw a man on horseback. White Bull said to interpreter, "There is a person who has seen us," and the interpreter told Gen. Miles. The Indian must have ridden fast back to camp, and the interpreter, after speaking to Gen. Miles, ran on to the little point near Gwalter's store [as of 1906] and came back, and then began the charge up as far as the first gulch below the camp where the troops stopped. By this time it was full daylight, but sun not up. When they stopped above roundhouse [1906], soldiers began to fire. Three men charged them from Lame Deer's camp. Then they could see the women and children run out of the lodges and strike for the hills. Some of the cavalry did not stop, but charged through the camp and got above it on the creek.

As they charged up the trail, the first soldier was killed just where Cooley's house is now [1906]. White Bull saw him fall from where he had been with Gen. Miles. Down near Lame Deer [Creek], in a bend of creek is a high bank 6 ft and 300 [?] yds east is a high knoll. Here Gen. Miles and White Bull stood. Bob Jackson was interpreter after Bruyer [Bruguier] had gone out with leading soldiers. Interpreter said, "This is Lame Deer's fight [camp?], and I bet that's Lame Deer over there now," pointing to an Indian man at a distance. Then Hump, who was back with infantry, rode up to the three on the knoll and said, "I will call down to these men and see what they say." The man who Jackson had said was Lame Deer had a white rag in his hand and raised it and all the shooting stopped. Then Hump called down to them asking them to surrender. The man was Lame Deer. Hump rode down to Lame Deer. Lame Deer's son was not still for a minute. He was walking up and down with his warbonnet on. Hump left Lame Deer and rode back to commanding officer. He said, "That is Lame Deer and he wants to see Gen. Miles." Gen. Miles had a white cloth tied around his head. He took off the white cloth and gave it to his orderly who took a white hat out of his saddle pocket and gave to general, who gave his gun to the orderly, but kept his pistol. Then they rode down to Lame Deer, eight in all. They kept approaching each other, Lame Deer, his son, and another Sioux, and another Sioux and a fourth Sioux leading Lame Deer's horse. When they came together, Lame Deer and Gen.

shook hands and Gen. Miles took off his hat. The son did not keep still. He walked up and down. The Sioux leading horse led it off toward creek. Gen. Miles said to interpreter, "Tell Lame Deer to put his gun down." Lame Deer put his gun on ground with muzzle toward Gen. Miles at full cock. Another Sioux did not put down his gun. The son walked up and down like a sentry outpost. The only thing he said was, "I am a soldier walking on my own land."

Gen. Miles did not notice the gun being at full cock and White Bull rode around close to Miles [and] pushed his leg with his foot, and when Miles looked around he made a motion with his mouth at the gun and signed that it was full cock. This put Gen. on his guard about the gun in case it should be picked up by Lame Deer. As they stood there, interpreter rode to White Bull and said to him, "You ride over to Lame Deer's son and tell him to surrender. Tell him to look at all women and children running to hills. Let him surrender. No one will be hurt and we will get in all the horses and bring them to the post." White Bull turned his horse, and as he turned interpreter said that Captain will help you. The captain and White Bull rode up to the son and White Bull spoke to him. He answered, "I told you once I am a soldier on my own ground," and he raised his gun and struck White Bull on the arm. White Bull spurred his horse close to him and caught the gun by the muzzle, and the captain caught the young man by the arm. They struggled for a moment and then White Bull pulled away the gun. In the struggle the gun went off, and the ball passed through White Bull's overcoat. He heard Lame Deer call out, "My friend is a young man." Then Lame Deer picked up his gun and fired at Gen. Miles. Gen. Miles threw himself to one side on his horse and the ball tore a big hole in his blouse.

Then everything turned loose. White Bull let go the gun and as he turned around he saw a sergeant Sharp draw his pistol and ride up to Lame Deer and shoot. Then Lame

Deer's son ran toward sergeant, who shot at him and then son shot at and hit the sergeant in breast. The sergeant's shot, White Bull thinks, killed the Sioux who was with the two. Then Gen Miles drew his pistol and fired at Lame Deer, who now started to walk away. All soon began to fire at Lame Deer, and the infantry came up on a charge. They kept moving, walking toward the hills where women and children were. Lame Deer said, "Turn and fight," but son was too weak. He was using his gun for a crutch or dragging it. They crossed Lame Deer [Creek] and went up a little gulch. White Bull and interpreter were close to them and soldiers and scouts were firing all the time. Lame Deer walked up to his son and took him by the shoulder, and just as he did so Lame Deer fell. The son turned and faced soldiers and fell sitting, bracing himself with his two hands. Then he tried to load his gun and succeeded, but he could not get it to his shoulder. As he sat there the interpreter Jackson knelt down and fired and the ball struck him in the middle of the forehead just cutting the lower edge of the browband of the warbonnet. He was a brave man to walk so far with such bad wounds as he had and not to give up his gun. He died with his gun in his hands. After the fight was over, White Bull scalped Lame Deer and son. The son was not Lame Deer's son but his nephew, the son of his brother. He was called Big Ankle which is said to have been also the name of the boy's father.[17]

While they were fighting here some young Sioux must have slipped around behind. Brave Eagle and some others charged the pack train of six mules which were behind. Killed one of the packers, captured the mules and the ammunition. That night after the fight, White Bull was called into Gen. Miles's tent. Gen. said to him, "Do you remember what I told you when you enlisted? Now these horses that we have taken you may have. And I want you always to keep this gun that you have been shooting at the

Sioux." He did keep it till it was burned in summer of 1905. He asked White Bull what he could do for him to pay for what he had done. White Bull said he wanted nothing except to be helped to continue to live in this country. White Bull had offered Ankle's scalp to Gen. Miles but he declined to take it.

He remembers that an officer killed a Sioux near forks of Lame Deer. Lame Deer was not then so named; it was called Muddy Creek. He knows of 5 Sioux killed, 2 women and 3 men. Others may have been killed above, about whom he did not know. Two soldiers were killed and one person—soldier or citizen—with the packtrain. The troops burnt and destroyed the village and ruined everything in it and took what they wanted. He got a lot of food, white grease, &c.

Yet another reminiscence of the Lame Deer fight was provided by the Minneconjou Hump, or High Backbone (1848–1907). Hump as a youth participated in many actions with enemy tribes. In 1876 he took part in the Little Big Horn battle, where he killed one soldier and captured four guns. A brave warrior and leader among his people, Hump saw the futility of continued resistance and in March 1877 was among those who surrendered to Miles at the Tongue River Cantonment. He enlisted as a scout for Miles and shortly thereafter accompanied the troops in the campaign against Lame Deer, also a Minneconjou. Hump's recollection affords the unique perspective of an Indian who chose to guide the soldiers against his own people, ostensibly because he realized the fruitlessness of prolonging the conflict and hoped to prevent a direct attack on Lame Deer's village. Hump's brief statement was given through Interpreter Giles Tapetola, May 8, 1905. It reposes in the South Dakota State Historical Society Collections in Pierre.

A DETACHMENT OF SOLDIERS and the Indian scouts went out to look for Chief Lame Deer and his band. Gen. N. Miles went along with us. I found the camp of Chief Lame Deer with his band near a creek, reported to the General

Hump, Minneconjou Lakota, 1890s. Photograph by R. L. Kelly. Courtesy of the South Dakota State Archives.

N. Miles and all the officers met in the evening and decided to surround the camp at night. But I told Gen. N. Miles if we do that, they will shoot us, but if you want to make peace and shake hands with them, we will make our appearance in daylight. He accepted my idea, so we went up to the camp in daylight and when we got near to the camp some of the Indian scouts and some of the Custer's survivors [Indian scouts for the army who had been with the Sioux and Cheyennes at Little Big Horn?] went up to the camp ahead of us to shake hands with the Chief Lame Deer. When we came in sight of Lame Deer's camp they were shooting each other. Whilst shooting each other, Gen. N. Miles wanted me to go to the Indians, so I went up and met three Indians, Chief Lame Deer, Ankle [Iron Star], [and] Roan Horse coming to see Bear Robe (N. Miles), and passing each other they went on to meet Bear Robe. They shook hands with Gen. N. Miles and after shaking hands with him Chief Lame Deer fired at the General but did not hurt him. The bullet only went through his uniform. This started the battle. The Indians stampeded and took refuge on a hill. Here Gen. N. Miles wanted me to go back to the Indians. But I refused it because they would kill me this time.

Chapter 12

The Death of Crazy Horse, September 5, 1877

Standing Soldier, Oglala Lakota; and American Horse, Oglala Lakota

For all practical purposes, the massive surrenders at the Dakota and Nebraska agencies in the spring and summer of 1877 marked the end of the Great Sioux War. Symbolically, however, two events ended the conflict—the movement of Sitting Bull's people into Canada in the spring of 1877 and the dramatic death of the thirty-five-year-old Oglala leader, Crazy Horse. From May until September following his surrender, Crazy Horse's presence at the Red Cloud Agency created turbulence and tension among the various factions of the Indians. A misunderstanding at a council in late August gave army officers the impression that the Oglala was to begin hostilities anew, thus precipitating his arrest. As Crazy Horse resisted imprisonment in the guardhouse at Camp Robinson, he received a bayonet wound that proved mortal.

The following accounts of the killing of Crazy Horse both agree and disagree, pointing up the controversy that surrounded the emotionally charged event. The Oglala Standing Soldier, at the time about twenty-six years old, witnessed the event at the guardhouse. His account was given to Ricker in 1906 and reposes in the Ricker Collection, Tablet 29, Microfilm Roll 5, Nebraska State Historical Society, Lincoln.

SPEAKING OF THE CAPTURE and death of Crazy Horse he [Standing Soldier] says that he was one of the scouts sent from Fort Robinson to Spotted Tail Agency to get him. When they got over to Spotted Tail they were told that Crazy Horse had said if anybody came after him he would kill him or them; so, it was arranged for some of the

Standing Soldier, Oglala Lakota, in 1906. Photograph by De-Lancey Gill. Courtesy of the South Dakota State Archives.

Rosebud Indians to go out and get him, which they did; and they took him under guard to Fort Robinson. The object in taking Crazy Horse was to convey him to Washington to see the president, and the agent at Red Cloud wanted the Rosebud Indians in charge to stop with him at the Agency so he would tell C. Horse the purpose for which he was being brought in and to have him left there, but they would not stop, but went on to the Fort where he was killed the same day. (I doubt whether he is correctly informed as to the object.)

An officer (and somebody else I have forgotten) and four privates went with Crazy Horse into the guard house followed by an Oglala, Little Big Man and some of Crazy Horse's friends. When inside, he saw where they were taking him, and he drew his knife and began backing out. Little Big Man shouted, "Don't! don't! don't do that!" and seized him by the arms. Crazy Horse cut Little Big Man in the wrist. The soldiers were trying to keep him in with their bayonets; he got out of doors and the guard on the outside stepped up and thrust his bayonet into his side low down and pretty well around toward his back. He fell and Standing Soldier lifted him up, but he was soon dead. The soldier stabbed him purposely. . . .

The recollection of American Horse was given to Eli S. Ricker on August 18, 1906. It is in the Ricker Collection, Tablet 35, Microfilm Roll 6, Nebraska State Historical Society, Lincoln.

AMERICAN HORSE AND ONE of his two wives and the daughter of this wife, having come with a large number of Indians to Chadron to take [railroad] cars for Cheyenne where they were to be an attraction on Pioneer Day, took dinner at my table, and American Horse gave us a description of the killing of Crazy Horse. In the struggle to escape from his captors he was held around the waist by an Indian who seized him from behind, while Little Big Man grasped his wrist and hands in which he held a knife. By turning his hand adroitly he gave Little Big Man a wound in his arm which caused him to release his hold, and thereupon making a violent effort to disengage himself he

American Horse, Oglala Lakota, in 1879. Photograph by H. Rocher. Courtesy of the Nebraska State Historical Society.

surged against a bayonet in the hands of one of the guards who was standing at a guard against infantry and swaying his piece forward and backward. The bayonet entered his side below the ribs inflicting a mortal wound.

American Horse positively affirms that the soldier did not stab Crazy Horse intentionally. He also said that he himself during the scuffle threw his gun down on Crazy Horse to shoot him, but some Indians pressed between them and prevented him from taking his life. So passed away one of the greatest Indian warriors of the later days.

Notes

1. *Battles and Skirmishes of the Great Sioux War, 1876–1877: The Military View* (Norman: University of Oklahoma Press, 1993).
2. This skirmish occurred on June 9, 1876, at a point where Prairie Dog Creek entered the Tongue.
3. Reference is to the military column from Fort Abraham Lincoln, commanded by Brigadier General Alfred H. Terry and including Lieutenant Colonel George A. Custer and the Seventh Cavalry. These troops were advancing up the Yellowstone River intent on meeting General Crook, coming from the south, as well as Colonel John Gibbon, coming from the west.
4. This inordinately high casualty count for the Indians is probably a translation error.
5. The pack train arrived after Reno had reached the hilltop.
6. This was Reno's attack on the south end of the Indian village.
7. The Indians, of course, did not at the time know the identity of the officer commanding the soldiers.
8. Flying By here means General Terry; Colonel Nelson A. Miles was known to the Indians as Bear Coat.
9. Indian losses at Slim Buttes numbered approximately ten killed and two wounded.
10. This is erroneous. The ponies were not recaptured.
11. There is perhaps a problem of interpretation here. Otis indeed met with representatives of Sitting Bull, but the Hunkpapa leader refused to appear.
12. Also known as Hanging Woman Creek.
13. Probably an error in interpretation. The fighting actually started early in the morning and lasted until noon—approximately five hours.

14. Miles's command numbered approximately 450 men.

15. This occurred on a butte situated on the east side of Tongue River, in an area east of the major concentration of soldiers.

16. Fort Keogh was completed in the summer of 1877, after the Lame Deer campaign. In May the troops still occupied the cantonment.

17. Big Ankle was also known as Iron Star.

Index

162 INDEX

Rising Sun, 106
Roan Horse, 147
Rosebud battlefield, 119
Rosebud Creek, 15, 16, 21, 23, 26, 27, 33, 35, 48, 49,
    61, 67, 75, 134–36, 139
Rosebud Creek, Battle of, 15–31, 49, 62
Rosebud Valley, 27
Rough Faces, 83
Rowland, Willis, 80, 114, 115
Runs-the-Bear, 128
Rushe's, 87

Sans Arc Lakota Indians, 17, 31, 33, 54, 88, 89, 93.
    See also Lakota Indians
Santee Dakota Indians, 33, 35
Scabby Island, 28
Second Cavalry, 9
Seventeenth Infantry, 98
Seventh Cavalry, 32, 34, 35, 153n.3
Sharp, Sergeant, 143
Sheridan, Wyo., 73
She Walks with Her Shawl, in Little Big Horn battle,
    40–46
Shoshoni Indians, 16, 19, 20, 114, 116, 120
Sibley, Frederick W., 73, 75
Sioux Indians. *See* Lakota Indians
Sitting Bear, 20
Sitting Bull, 14, 16, 17, 31, 42, 53, 54, 56, 58, 59, 85,
    93, 96–98, 105, 109, 125, 148, 153n.11; in Cedar
    Creek councils, 100–103, 106–107, 112
Sitting Bull-the-Good, 111
Slim Buttes, 85–89
Slim Buttes, battle of, 58, 85–90, 92, 93, 153n.9
Slohan, 42
Snake Indians, 121. *See also* Shoshoni Indians
Soldier, 87
Soldier Wolf, in Little Big Horn battle, 51–52
South Dakota, 42, 59, 85
Split, 87